1⁵⁰

Quito
apostles,
woven

Paul

EDGAR J. GOODSPEED

Paul

THE JOHN C. WINSTON COMPANY

♦ PHILADELPHIA ♦ TORONTO ♦

To Harold Lamb
*Gifted portrayer of great figures of the past
and understanding and inspiring friend*

ACKNOWLEDGMENTS

Acknowledgment is gratefully made to the University of Chicago Press for permission to use the text of *The Bible, An American Translation*, in quoting the Old and New Testaments. My brother, Charles T. B. Goodspeed, has again come to my assistance by giving the proofs of this book an independent reading.

PREFACE

Paul was a great man. He was a man of action, moving about the Roman Empire to make the Christian gospel known to Jews and Greeks just as far as he could possibly travel. He died with his eyes fixed on distant Spanish shores he never reached. He had a genius for friendship. He was a welcome guest in the homes of the first century. His converts were his friends, and if they sometimes seemed to disown his friendship, it reduced him to the depths of discouragement and almost to despair.

He was also a thinker, capable of thinking a problem through to some great deciding principle. We are fortunate in possessing in perhaps a dozen letters from his hand glimpses of the thoughts that filled his mind at as many points in his career, a boon indeed to his biographers, who are not wholly dependent on what other men thought about him, but can see in his letters what he himself was thinking.

The biographer of Paul thus sets himself to weave the letters into the narrative of The Acts as the weaver weaves his threads into the warp on his loom. It is his task to bring him back as he moved among men, a man of vision, power and conviction, dealing with people very much like ourselves, but dealing with their problems and weaknesses with such extraordinary patience, penetration and understanding that what he said to them can still guide and instruct us, even in this late day, and teach our generation lessons of faith, tolerance, love and courage it still greatly needs to learn.

CONTENTS

I A Boy in Tarsus 1
II Paul Changes Worlds 10
III First Steps in a New World 20
IV Finding His Task 29
V Penetrating the Greek World . . . 38
VI Leadership in Galatia 46
VII An International Religion 54
VIII Christianity Enters Europe 65
IX Thessalonica to Athens 81
X Great Days in Corinth 90
XI Report to Antioch 102
XII The Gospel in Ephesus 113
XIII Controversy with Corinth 128
XIV Reconciliation with Corinth . . . 138
XV Looking Westward 145
XVI Turning Eastward 155
XVII Crisis at Jerusalem 163
XVIII A Prisoner in Palestine 173
XIX The Great Voyage 187
XX From a Roman Prison 199
XXI The Return of Paul 212
Chronology 222
Notes 223
Books About Paul 240

CHAPTER 1 ❧ A BOY IN TARSUS

VERY EARLY in the history of the Christian movement there came a time when it seemed in danger of withering into just another of the sects of Judaism, such as the Pharisees, Sadducees, Essenes and Zealots. But one man appeared who saw in it far more than that, and beyond any of his contemporaries perceived and championed its great rôle as a world religion. His name was Paul.

For about fifteen years after the birth of Jesus in Bethlehem another boy was born in a Jewish home out in the Roman Empire who was destined to exert a twofold influence of great range and power on behalf of the new Christian faith, first by his missionary travels and then a generation later by the letters he had written, when they were collected and published. Other men traveled and other men wrote, but none performed both these services to the new faith to the extent that he did. And of all the followers of Jesus, none made so great a contribution to the thinking of mankind as Paul.

It is by that Roman name that history knows him. But the name his Hebrew parents gave him when on the eighth day of his life he was circumcised and, as we would say, christened, was the Hebrew name Saul.

The long reign of Augustus, the first emperor of Rome (31 B.C.–A.D. 14) was drawing to a close. It had been a great period in the history and civilization of the countries about the Mediterranean. He had enlarged the empire, organized its twenty-seven provinces under governors responsible to Rome, and introduced an era of peace, prosperity and order such as most of them had never known before. But the next reign, that of Tiberius, was to witness the dawn of a new movement, in which Saul, or Paul, was to bear an important part. In fact, he was going to be remembered and influential beyond almost any man of his generation, except Jesus himself.

Paul was born about A.D. 10–15, in the ancient city of Tarsus, the capital of Cilicia. A thousand years of history lay behind it, and its population in Paul's day probably approached half a million people. At Tarsus the old trade route from the east made contact with the Mediterranean and turned north through the Taurus mountains into the uplands of Asia Minor. The road over the mountains followed a river bed, which was often impassable, and the Tarsians, with an engineering enterprise which we like to think modern, and which was unusual in antiquity, had chiseled a highway out of the cliff beside the river, forming the Cilician Gates, one of the most famous passes in the ancient world.

Cilicia was a narrow province, from thirty to sixty miles wide and perhaps three hundred miles long, lying between the Taurus mountains and the Mediterranean, and forming the eastern half of the southern coast of Asia Minor. Tarsus was its great commercial center, for the Cydnus River ran through the city, and the lake the river formed a few miles below the city had been made into the harbor of Tarsus, to which ships came from all over the Mediterranean. Up this river Cleopatra had sailed in her splendid galley to meet and captivate Antony, in 41 B.C.

The victories of Alexander the Great, who entered Tarsus in 334 B.C., brought many Greek residents to the old town, and it became very much of a Greek city, with all the features of Greek city life, including a thriving university. In it the Stoic Athenodorus of Tarsus, so long the teacher and adviser of Augustus, lectured in his later years. It was Athenodorus who advised the emperor when he was angry to repeat the alphabet before he said or did anything. Athenodorus was the scholar in politics, for when he came back to Tarsus in 15 B.C. and found the city controlled by a corrupt machine, he turned it out of office and sent its members into exile.

The Jews had been brought into Tarsus, too, especially in 171 B.C., when the assurance of the rights of citizenship led many Jews to take up their residence there. It was probably from one of these that Paul had inherited his citizenship in Tarsus, in which he took a natural pride. Even more important was the Roman citizenship, to which he appealed in one crisis of his life, declaring that he possessed it by inheritance.

It was the synagogue rather than the university that was to influence Paul, and his bringing up was strictly Jewish. Both his parents were Hebrews, and he traced his ancestry back through the tribe of Benjamin to the younger son of Jacob and Rachel. He was circumcised the eighth day, as the Law prescribed, and named Saul (Sha'ul) after the old Benjamite hero Saul, the first king of Israel. As a Roman citizen, he had to have a full Roman name, first, second and third (prænomen, nomen and cognomen), but the Greeks, with whom he principally labored in after years, used only one name; they spoke of Plato, Socrates, Aristotle. So Saul came to be known by his cognomen Paulus, or, as we call him, Paul.

From childhood Paul heard and used Aramaic at home, but Tarsus was a Greek city, and in its shops and streets he learned Greek almost as soon. His people were Pharisees of the strictest kind, and all the numerous provisions of Pharisaic legalism were rigidly observed in his home. Many of these still survive among orthodox Jews in this day. On the Sabbath anything remotely resembling work of any kind was avoided, and the Levitical ceremonial laws about clean and unclean foods were rigidly observed. In a Pharisaic home, Paul must have begun the study of the Law at an early age and become proficient in Hebrew.[1] In the synagogue he would hear the entire Law read through in Hebrew in the course of three years, and the prophets, "former" and "latter," were read there too. The Greek version of the Jewish Scriptures, and some Jewish writings in Greek, Paul would come to know. But Greek literature in general would have little interest for a boy of Pharisaic upbringing, brought up to believe that he already "had knowledge and truth formulated in the Law."

We cannot say that the university influenced Paul's youth; he was probably brought up with a Pharisee's abhorrence for pagan culture. But he grew up in a Greek city in which Jews, Greeks and Orientals lived together more harmoniously than almost anywhere else, and later on when he had occasion to write to his Greek friends he knew how to express himself with ease and vigor in the Greek of the common dialect. Yet when he faced the Jewish mob in Jerusalem from the barracks steps, he spoke to them in their native Aramaic.

Since Paul inherited his Roman citizenship, his father must have been a Roman citizen before him, and must have been a man of position in the city. Certainly the family, with both Tarsian and Roman citizenship, was a prominent one. They believed in the Roman Empire, which had brought such definite material benefits to their world. Peace and order, bridges, roads and aqueducts were spreading over the world. Its laws were to be obeyed, and its demands met; they were its loyal subjects, not its sullen slaves. They saw in the officers of the empire the agents of the will of God. Certainly these were the views of Paul in later years. It is evident that his family had not suffered at the hands of the empire and took the most favorable possible view of it, at a time when some Jewish groups in Palestine were fomenting resistance and rebellion. Paul, and probably his father before him, was empire-conscious; Paul always calls the parts of the empire by their proper provincial names, not their older local ones, which Luke generally uses. These attitudes of Paul's toward the Roman Empire combine with his Roman name Paulus to confirm Luke's statement that he was a Roman citizen, like his father before him.

Apart from this we know almost nothing about Paul's family. The highest compliment he can pay to the mother of Rufus is to say that she has been a mother to him. But all he has to suggest to the fathers of Colossæ is, "Fathers, do not irritate your children, or they may lose heart." Paul had certainly seen cases of such paternal irritation; he may even have experienced it, but it would be unjust to think this line a portrait of his father, stern old Pharisee and pillar of the synagogue as he doubtless was. Certainly Paul has no nobler term to apply to God than Abba, the Aramaic word for father, with which he no doubt familiarly addressed his own father in his youth in Tarsus.

Paul may have had a number of brothers and sisters, but we know of only one, for when he was arrested by the Romans in Jerusalem, a nephew of his, the son of his sister, was residing there. This young man was in such contact with the most turbulent Jewish element there that he was able to warn Paul that he was in danger of being mobbed by them. When this warning was communicated to the Roman colonel in charge of Paul, that officer had him removed to Cæsarea for safety. This nephew was evidently still friendly to his uncle, notwithstanding Paul's Christian profession.

The "kinsmen" Paul mentions in Romans—Andronicus, Junias, Herodion, Lucius, Jason and Sosipater—were not his relatives, but simply men of Jewish blood, or perhaps members of the same Jewish "tribe" with Paul in the Roman organization of Tarsus.

Paul looked back upon a normal childhood: When he was a child, he told the Corinthians long after, he talked like a child, thought like a child, and reasoned like a child. Yet he must have been a boy of extraordinary sensitiveness, alertness and vivacity. Certainly he came to feel an intense devotion to the Jewish Law, the great religious inheritance of Judaism, and in his early manhood this devotion developed into positive fanaticism.

His people were Pharisees and, with the other members of that party, accepted not only the books of Moses, Genesis to Deuteronomy, but the prophets and the "writings" as Scripture. So Paul grew up in the presence of what we know as the Old Testament, or the most of it. He heard it constantly interpreted, debated and praised. His mind was stored with it, and his letters, written long after, were enriched with scores of quotations and echoes of its books, more than half of which are reflected in his writings. The Hebrew Scriptures had become part of his mental furnishings, not at all for their literary or rhetorical value, but for their religious usefulness, and as the adequate intellectual expression of truth and knowledge.

Paul was brought up to be a Jew and to be proud of it. It came back to him in after years, when he was writing to the Romans. What a splendid heritage Israel had! To them belonged all the rights of sonship, God's glorious presence, the divine agreement and legislation, the Temple service, the promises and the patriarchs! He felt it still, as a Christian apostle, as he had come to feel it as a youth in Tarsus. Obviously, there was never anything half-hearted about Paul.

In somewhat later times, the Jewish youth program was definitely fixed: at five, the boy came to the reading of Scripture, at ten to the Mishna, at thirteen to the practice of the commands, at fifteen to the Talmud, at eighteen to marriage, and something like this was very probably about what was expected of Paul, though Mishna and Talmud had not taken shape in his day. Certainly at thirteen he would be expected to observe the Law, and in the synagogue would no longer sit with his mother in a gallery or behind a screen, but would take his place with the men of Israel and raise his voice in the psalms and prayers of the service.

The observance of the Law of Moses as the Pharisees saw it was a serious and engrossing business. They regarded it as the full and adequate expression of the will of God. They accepted not only the Law in all its details, but for safety's sake threw about it a fence of refinements and safeguards, so that there could be no mistake about observing it. This mass of decisions, the Halakhah, was later codified in the Mishna. They must do no work on the Sabbath, but just how much activity could be indulged in, short of what was meant by work? How far could one go on the Sabbath without traveling? How much wheat could one pluck without reaping, or strip of the chaff without threshing? How many stitches could one take without sewing? These were matters of real concern to the conscientious Pharisee, if he was to please God.

So Paul grew up wedded to a great system of minute details of conduct, on the one hand, while he tried to keep step with the giant strides of the Hebrew prophets on the other. There was a profound disunion in his religious attitudes from his youth up, whether or not he was aware of it. Was religion and the service of God the painstaking observance of a set of petty rules, or was it a great spiritual experience of the love and mercy of God? Could it be both?

At the same time, Jews and Gentiles got on together better in Tarsus than in almost any other great city in the Roman Empire. How much contact Paul had with Tarsus boys not of Jewish blood we cannot say; he would not meet them in school or synagogue, and his playfellows were probably Jewish like himself. And yet he came to have a consciousness of people about him who were not Jews that made him ready in after years to take the lead in opening the Christian circle to them as well as to Jews. Certainly he learned their language, the common dialect Greek so widely spoken all the way to Rome itself. This was to prove of enormous value to him in later years, when with the utmost vigor and freedom he preached and wrote to Greeks in their own tongue all over the eastern empire.

S AUL WAS a sensitive, conscientious, devout, enthusiastic and very gifted boy, and it was early felt that he ought to be given the best possible education and become a rabbi. For while the Paulus family were loyal Roman citizens, they were also pious Jews and zealous Pharisees who felt that the study of the Jewish Law was the highest of callings. So Saul was early destined for a rabbinical training. The center of such studies was, of course, Jerusalem, and Saul was sent there to study. In later years he had a nephew, his sister's son, in Jerusalem, and he may already have had a married sister living there, in whose house he could live while he carried on his studies under Gamaliel, the leading rabbi of the day. Gamaliel was the grandson of the famous Hillel, a leader of the more humane school of Judaism in such matters as divorce, Sabbath observance, and relations with the heathen. In later days Gamaliel was rated the first of the seven "rabbans," or rabbis of especial distinction. Josephus began his serious course of Pharisaic study at twenty, and Saul may have been about that age when he went to Jerusalem to study under Gamaliel, as so many of us nowadays leave home to go to college.

The Jewish rabbi had to have a trade by which he could earn his living, so that he could teach his people without being paid for it, and no doubt before Saul left Tarsus he had learned his trade. He had learned to work in the rough "Cilician cloth" made of goat's hair, which had taken its name "cilicium" from the province of Cilicia. But it was even then an ancient material, for in Exodus the outer covering of the Tabernacle is described as made of goat's hair. Saul could make the fabric or work it into the tents, sails and awnings made of it that were so well known in the Roman world. Such tents were used in the Roman army. Saul was a good workman at this trade, for he seems to have had no difficulty in getting a job wherever he settled for any length of time, anywhere about the Ægean. The Jews fully realized that the ability to earn one's living was the surest way to economic security, and all his life Paul preferred to earn his living by practicing his trade. True to his rabbinic training, he would never accept pay for teaching, but only for his skill at his trade. This became long after one of his chief differences with the Corinthians, who could not understand such an attitude. Certainly mastering such a trade was a necessary step in Saul's preparation to be a rabbi.

Pharisaism had its beginnings in the Maccabean times when the threat of persecution was driving many Jews to relinquish their distinctive manner of life and accept Greek ways. The First Book of Maccabees tells the story. They were called upon to eat pork, and renounce the food laws of Leviticus, to give up their copies of the Law to their persecutors, and let the Temple be profaned and their children go uncircumcised. But some stoutly refused to accede to these demands, preferring at whatever sacrifice or peril to separate themselves from the rest and declare their complete devotion to the service of God. They professed to be his people, holy men, saints of God, with no other purpose in life than to carry out his will as revealed in the Law. So arose the Pharisees, as the Puritans of Judaism, its professed "saints." This term Paul carried on into his Christian period, since he felt that the Christian believer was similarly devoted to the service of God, and one of God's people. This was the nobler side of Pharisaism and gave expression in Paul's day to what was best in Judaism. Its weakness lay in its tendency to direct the Pharisee's attention not to spiritual fellowship with God, but to the written Law as a full expression of his will, so that religion became not a great inward experience but the meticulous performance of a technique. Further, since it assumed that the Law was the full expression of the will of God, it envisaged the possibility that a man might carry it out so completely that God himself could ask no more of him. Since ordinary people could not possibly carry out the ceremonial Law with the fulness the Pharisee thought necessary, they came to be considered by him "sinners"—irreligious people, whose future was hopeless. The superiority the Pharisee felt in relation to them inevitably beguiled him into spiritual pride, and the Pharisees degenerated into a sort of spiritual aristocracy, obsessed by their own pretensions of superiority.

There was, of course, a much harsher Pharisaism, of the kind Jesus encountered in the centers of Galilee, the kind that is reflected in II Maccabees and condemned in the Sermon on the Mount. It was the kind that really hated its enemies, like the slain Nicanor, whose tongue it vauntingly proposed to cut in little pieces and feed to the birds. It is this last page of that Pharisaic book that is too often forgotten in modern efforts to picture the first-century Pharisee.

It is not difficult to find all these aspects of Pharisaism warring in the troubled heart of Saul the Pharisee. What he did and what he afterwards wrote about his own spiritual experience in Judaism show us the nobler as well as the harsher and the more trivial elements of Pharisaism, and one man's heroic, even desperate, effort to carry out its tenets to their fullest expression. But it all ended in unrest and disappointment. Saul felt his heart, his inmost attitudes, unreached by all these minutiæ of detail as to ceremonial cleanness and Sabbath observance, and the religious sterility of it all sometimes almost drove him to despair. "Wretched man that I am!" he thought. "Who can save me from this doomed body?" But he stormed on, hoping that perhaps more frantic efforts might bring him through to the light.

The immensely broader and deeper view of religion championed by Jesus was especially attractive to Hellenistic Jews, that is, Jews born and brought up out in the great cities of the Greco-Roman world, to which many Jews had moved to make a better living. Such Jews knew something of the thought and life of the great world of their day. One of these was Stephen, the first of the seven deacons who were very early chosen by believers in Jerusalem to relieve the apostles of the business side of the movement. The activities of Stephen, however, were not confined to supervising the charities of the church, for he very soon became involved in religious discussions with other Hellenists in Jerusalem. These became so sharp that they attracted the attention of the supreme Jewish council, the Sanhedrin, and

Stephen was called before that body to defend himself. His insistence upon the spiritual nature of religion, coupled with bitter denunciation of the Jews for always refusing the leaders God sent them, was interpreted by that tribunal as blasphemy, and he was dragged out of the city to less sacred ground and there cruelly stoned to death, as prescribed by the laws of Leviticus and Deuteronomy.[1] Stephen thus became the first martyr of the new movement, and his dramatic death marked an important step in the progress of the new faith from being just another sect of Judaism to becoming a new religion.

Paul first appears upon the stage of history as Saul, the young man at whose feet the killers of Stephen threw down their clothes as they stripped for their work.[2] He is spoken of almost as if he had some official relation to what was done; certainly he was no mere bystander. The witnesses of what they considered Stephen's blasphemy identified themselves to him as they stripped off their outer garments for their cruel work. Already Saul was a zealous Pharisee, deeply concerned for the preservation and the observance of the Jewish Law. The stoning of Stephen must have appeared to Saul simply a carrying out of the law of Deuteronomy against apostates and idolaters. There had to be two or three witnesses, and these must be the first to stone the guilty man or woman.[3]

This was probably the first violent death Saul had ever witnessed. He would not have attended the gladiatorial shows which the heathen masses so enjoyed under Roman civilization. Augustus in his famous summary of his reign, his great epitaph, the Res Gestae, declared with pride that in the gladiatorial shows he had given, ten thousand men had fought. Of course, most of them had been killed, before enormous crowds gathered in vast amphitheaters. Stoning was a peculiarly brutal and revolting form of execution, intended to put the whole congregation back of the deed, in which all were expected to share. Nor was it witnessed as a spectacle, from a distance; it was done close at hand, with clumsy violence, in bitter rage. There were no onlookers; all were expected to participate and thus to share in the responsibility. The hands of the witnesses were to be the first against him to put him to death, and then the hands of all the people; so ran the law of Deuteronomy. It was all a hideous survival from primitive times, brutalizing those who participated in it, one of whom must have been Saul himself. Indeed, he probably gave the signal for it to begin, when the requisite witnesses had identified themselves to him. It was a dreadful experience for any man, and doubly so for Saul, who was haunted by the memory of it in after years.

Christians remembered that when Stephen faced the council to begin his defense, his face was like an angel's, and that he died asking God to forgive his murderers. Who is so likely to have told Luke of these things as Saul himself? Certainly The Acts gives us the impression that he often spoke with remorse of his persecution of the church.[4]

That the witnesses reported, as it were, to Saul before throwing their stones makes it appear that Saul, if not himself a member of the Jewish council, or Sanhedrin, was its representative at the execution of Stephen, for though in Roman eyes it was the act of a mob, from a strictly Jewish point of view it was simply the carrying out of a higher law.

Certainly a Pharisee would have thought so. Saul was probably not a member of the Sanhedrin, for he is called a young man, and the Sanhedrin was modeled upon the council of seventy elders described in Numbers as assembled by Moses at God's command in the desert of Sinai. These elders were presumably the heads of families, and we do not know that Paul ever married; in fact in later years in his letters he intimates that he had not.[5]

It is impossible to resist the conclusion that in Jerusalem, despite the influence of Gamaliel, Saul fell under fanatical nationalist influences and lost the sense of loyalty to Rome and Roman law with which he had grown up and to which he later returned. His student days in Jerusalem must have witnessed the development of a bitter opposition in his breast between his acceptance of membership in the Roman Empire and membership in the Jewish people, and particularly in the party of the Pharisees. Not that the Pharisees were revolutionists. From Maccabean times they had been the ones who sought only religious freedom, and were not concerned for political independence. Nor did the attack on Stephen have any direct political significance. But under Roman domination the council had no right to execute Stephen, and in taking part in his execution Saul had disobeyed the Roman authority. He had followed the Law of Moses in violation of the laws of Rome.

Saul's share in this affair increased his standing with the high priest, but it must have caused him grave misgivings and left an indelible mark upon his conscience. He was passing through a time of great inward turmoil and confusion, such as is in part reflected in his discussion long afterwards of sin and law in the sixth and seventh chapters of Romans. And as if seeking relief in action from his bewildering moral problems, Saul the eager young Pharisee stormed on. From supervising the hideous death of Stephen it was a natural step to carry his fanatical campaign into wider fields. The followers of Jesus were still only a sect of Judaism, and they must be exterminated.

The zeal and efficiency Saul had shown in connection with the death of Stephen led to his being commissioned to carry out a house-to-house search for other followers of Jesus in Jerusalem. The council could not safely kill them, but there were other penalties it could inflict, in the way of beatings and imprisonments. The leaders of the new faith were forced to flee from Jerusalem, and the Jewish authorities took measures to follow them to neighboring cities.

So it was with letters from the high priest that Saul set out for Damascus to carry out an inquisition there, and if any believers could be found to bring them back to Jerusalem.

The Acts describes Saul as breathing murderous threats against the disciples as he left Jerusalem, and such extravagance of manner often cloaks a bewildered and agonized uncertainty. Certainly Saul's cherished Law had betrayed him into one terrible experience in the affair of Stephen, doubly disturbing to a man as sensitive and kindly as Saul must naturally have been to be capable of becoming the Paul of later years. Yet he was not ready to turn back, and there seemed no way to go but forward, to more such scenes of brutality and violence. If it was indeed the will of God, Saul should be able to get accustomed to it.

PAUL

The journey to Damascus must have taken a week, mounted as Saul and his companions doubtless were; a perplexed and agonized week for him. How he must have dreaded the moment of his arrival in Damascus, where he must again become the agent of cruelty and bigotry and act the hateful part of grand inquisitor!

As he drew near the city, his anguish of spirit increased. Was this then really the will of God, persecution and cruelty, baptized with the holy name of religion? Must he go on implementing it against humble, earnest people whose humility and heroism rebuked his arrogance and pride? Who was this Jesus, against whom he must so bitterly crusade in the name of God? It was midday and his figure rose before the mind of Saul, reproachful and sublime. And suddenly Saul saw him in a new light, not an impostor and upstart to be condemned and persecuted but a master and leader who could deliver him from all his confusion and pain. It burst upon him with all the suddenness of a revelation, turning his world over and restoring his moral values to their rightful place. It challenged him with the clearness of an audible voice: "Saul! Saul! Why do you persecute me?" Why, why indeed was he persecuting Jesus? He should be following him.

Paul himself said of this experience in after years that God had revealed his Son to him. And his conversion remains the most conspicuous example of a complete and instantaneous about-face in religion. One moment Saul was moving toward Damascus to organize a persecution of the believers there. The next, he was a believer himself, ready to sit at the disciples' feet and learn more of the way of Christ.

Saul had been following with great earnestness a religious course which was growing more and more distasteful and repugnant to him. It must have gone against the grain with a man so sensitive that he could afterwards write the thirteenth chapter of I Corinthians and the fourteenth chapter of Romans, those classics of love and tolerance, to be persecuting the church and ravaging it, as Paul in Galatians described himself as doing. He was indeed a different man when he wrote those letters, but those basic capacities had been his from the beginning. Other strong men have been known to follow a course of dogmatism that grew more and more intense as they pursued it until it became a burden that could no longer be borne, and they threw it off and turned away from it completely.

It was the conviction of the Early Church that the vision of Christ and acceptance of him released new powers in the believer, and never was this truer than in the case of Paul. He was a man of great intellectual gifts, but under the yoke of Pharisaic Judaism there was no scope for their employment. The Pharisee was estopped from the full, free exercise of his mind by tradition and authority; as a Pharisee Saul could do little but repress and stifle the capacities latent within him. What place was there in orthodox Judaism for the brilliance, originality and force he showed later? It had no field, no room. All he could hope to do was to search out and reaffirm the sayings of the rabbis or the ordinances of Moses. Saul's conversion was not only a spiritual emancipation; it was a great intellectual release. Not only his spirit but his mind was set free!

CHAPTER III ✺ FIRST STEPS IN A NEW WORLD

THEY STILL point out in Damascus the "street called Straight," where Saul found refuge in the days of prostration and blindness that followed his shattering experience as he approached the city. He had suddenly seen not only his religion but himself in a new light. Instead of being all right, as the Pharisee believed himself to be, in doctrine and conduct, he was all wrong. It was a mistake to be hounding the humble followers of Jesus, and as for killing Stephen, so far from being a thing to be proud of, it was a mistake, a crime and, worst of all, a sin. Instead of being competent to guide the blind, enlighten those in the dark, train the foolish, and teach the young, as the Jew liked to consider himself,[1] he was himself blind and ignorant and guilty! This was a terrific awakening. Saul's religious pride burst like a bubble. Not only did his idea of his religion and of himself go overboard, even his idea of God was transformed. He was swept from all his old moorings, and left with nothing to cling to but the vision he had had of Jesus, who had somehow gotten into his heart and taken possession.

No wonder his companions had to lead him by the hand into Damascus. Dazed as he was, he could not eat or see. He could only pray. News of his arrival and of his experience spread among the Jews and Jewish Christians there. His letters of introduction were, of course, to the synagogues, but it was among the Christians that he found the sympathy and companionship he so greatly needed. Certainly it was one of these named Ananias who came to see him, gave him reassurance, and welcomed him to the Christian fellowship. Saul got up from his bed, accepted baptism and joined the brotherhood.

Paul himself, in the invaluable account of his movements that he gives in Galatians, tell us that he went from Damascus to Arabia, that vast arid country stretching from Damascus to Mount Sinai, the Red Sea and the Persian Gulf. To some retreat on a near-by oasis Paul must have gone, to begin a tremendous inner reconstruction of his religious thinking. For he had not just lightly added Jesus to his Jewish theology, as the Messiah foretold by the prophets; he had seen in him the transformation of his whole religious world. Law, Scripture, tradition, ceremonial, the corner stones of his theology and practice must be rigorously reëxamined, in the light of his new religious experience. How drastically and honestly this was done his letters still show. It was all faithfully subordinated to the testimony of his own inward experience of faith; that stood supreme. Other Christian thinkers like Peter who still clung half-heartedly to the old Jewish food requirements found themselves left behind by Paul's bold, thoroughgoing abandonment of it all. Hebrew privilege, the supremacy of the Law, the externality of religion, the authority of tradition, scribal interpretation—of these and many other cherished positions of Judaism and Pharisaism Paul cleared his spiritual house, beginning in that significant period of silence and seclusion in Arabia.

During these months of recuperation and readjustment

on some Arabian oasis, Paul was far from idle. He was launched on his greatest voyage of spiritual exploration and discovery. He knew at last what it was to be free, and his lofty spirit and brilliant mind together reached forth to new heights and attitudes. Here began that extraordinary religious progress unsurpassed, unequaled even, in all the subsequent story of Christianity, which in every age has found strength and guidance in the findings of Paul. Some, at least, of its chief aspects we can recapture from the letters he afterwards wrote; repentance, redemption, forgiveness, tolerance, faith, hope, love—these were the experiences that flooded in upon his heart. Great thoughts came with them: freedom, sonship, salvation, eternal life. He had broken through to the presence of eternal reality, or it had broken through to him.

A man of emotion may change his whole attitude in an instant, but a thinker must have time to reconstruct his inner world. Changed though he was in point of view, Paul needed such a period as this retreat into Arabia afforded him. But when the months there were over, he turned back to his original destination, Damascus. He might have passed that city by, but he felt a responsibility to the believers there that he could not neglect. He had come to hunt out and persecute them; he must return there to support and strengthen them instead. The synagogues he had come to clear of the believers in the new faith he now entered not as the persecutor of that faith but as its champion. The relief and gratification of the Christians was only equaled by the vexation and dismay of the Jews, for Saul's vigorous and well-stored mind discovered arguments for Jesus' Messiahship far beyond those which other Christian thinkers had yet found. He was trained to be a Pharisaic rabbi; the religious treasures of the Jewish Scriptures lay before his mind, Moses, the prophets, and the writings, with all their varied wealth of religious experience and aspiration. Their letter he had indeed found dead, but filled as he now was with the new, life-giving spirit he saw in them other and greater values. Why, this new experience of faith that had filled his heart to overflowing, this attitude of penitence, trust, obedience and love, was just what had moved Abraham long ago and made him acceptable to God at the very outset of Hebrew religious history. It was indeed as if scales had fallen from Saul's eyes.

At first the synagogues were open to him. The believers were still synagogue-goers, Jewish Messianists, though of a more intense type than others. Now, in the hands of Paul, the rift between the new views and their old Pharisaic Judaism with its legalism, its scribal tradition, and its formalism became clearer, and some of them found the new faith irresistibly attractive. But to most of the Jews all this was doubly offensive. They had regarded Saul as an ally and a reinforcement, and he had turned out quite the opposite. In their eyes he was nothing less than a renegade. His success in his advocacy of the new cause in their synagogues intensified this animosity to the point of fury. The same violence Paul had meted out to Stephen must be applied to him. There was even a strange poetic justice in this situation. If Stephen had deserved stoning then, Paul deserved it now. So the Jews reasoned, and took their measures to act upon their reasoning.

In the long catalog of hardships suffered in his missionary work which Paul gives in II Corinthians, he makes the astounding statement that on five occasions he had been given thirty-nine lashes, the maximum penalty of the kind, by the Jews.[2] It is impossible to identify these occasions; the narrative of Acts does not mention them. But there is every reason to believe his work among the Jews of Damascus culminated in his first experience of this painful and humiliating kind. They could not stone him, but they could flog him, taking care not to exceed the maximum of forty lashes fixed by Deuteronomy.[3] It was Jewish practice to stop at thirty-nine, for fear of miscounting and thus unwittingly breaking the Law.

Such an action by one of the Damascus synagogues must have preceded the final scene in Paul's strange visit to that city. Flogging was bad enough, but worse was probably in store for him, and he must have gone into hiding among the Damascus believers who were now his devoted friends. But he could not remain hidden in Damascus always, and his Jewish enemies saw that when he tried to leave the city he could be seized and killed.

What followed remained in his memory the most dramatic of all his escapes. Damascus was, of course, a walled city, and it was easy enough to guard the few gates, one of which, a stately structure almost forty feet high, with three archways, still stands from the Roman period. It is interesting as one of the gates by which Paul did *not* leave Damascus. For the Jews there had made their arrangements with the governor under the Nabatean king Aretas, who for almost fifty years, 9 B.C. to A.D. 40, ruled Arabia, that Paul was not to be allowed to leave the city, but was to be taken into custody if he tried to do so.

Damascus had previously been in Roman hands, but Roman coins of Damascus stop with A.D. 34 and do not resume until nearly thirty years later, so that by A.D. 35 Aretas IV was probably once more in possession. It was his representative whom the Jews had convinced that Paul was a dangerous man who must not be allowed to get away.

Things must have looked very black indeed for Paul. He was beginning to live dangerously, with a vengeance. But he was always a resourceful man, and under cover of darkness his Christian friends smuggled him into a room on the outer wall, not too near a gate, and lowered him in a basket from a window in the wall. So he escaped with his life from his first Christian adventure, a foretaste of a long series that were to come.

Modern Damascus still has about a mile of city wall on its eastern side, and in it is shown the window from which you are told Paul made his perilous descent and escape. But, of course, the old Roman walls are now almost gone; only their foundations remain, supporting Arab and Turkish layers of superstructure. And yet it may well have been from this eastern side of the city, exactly opposite the natural exit for Jerusalem and the west, that Paul made his escape.

His Christian friends must have thought of his departure with great anxiety. Would he elude the watchers on the roads and get away in safety? If he did not, history would be different, much more different than they could have dreamed. There would have been no Pauline missionary journeys, no Pauline letters, to guide Christian life and thought for centuries, and no Pauline contribution to human thinking. A world of consequences hung on that slender rope that supported Paul's basket as he swung for a minute or two there in the darkness against the outer wall of Damascus. It was in every way an anxious moment for him and them, and for the Christian cause.

Safely out of Damascus, Paul made his way back to Jerusalem.[4] What with his months of reflection and reconstruction in Arabia and the months he had spent later in Damascus, some two or three years had passed since he had left Jerusalem on his errand for the high priest. He was a very different man from the Saul of Tarsus who had persecuted the church, and the Jerusalem to which he returned was to him now a very different city. His old friends and sponsors there were now his foes, but his former foes were not yet ready to be his friends. Word went around among them that he was now preaching the faith they held, but they found it hard to believe that he was really a disciple like themselves. It was a brother named Barnabas, a Jew from the island of Cyprus, not far from Tarsus, who made friends with Paul and vouched for him. Perhaps he had heard from Damascus and knew what Paul had done for the cause there; Paul may have brought letters from the Christians there. But the death of Stephen had made an indelible impression upon the believers in Jerusalem, and they found Paul's participation in it hard to forgive or forget.

Barnabas succeeded in introducing Paul to Peter and to Jesus' brother James. Jesus' family did not join his followers until after the crucifixion, and James, evidently the eldest of his brothers, soon came to the front among the Jerusalem believers and remained the leader of the church there as long as he lived.

But it was Paul's interviews with Peter that impressed him most deeply. It must have been an extraordinary meeting. The unschooled fisherman from Galilee, whom contact with Jesus had raised to such heights of experience and influence, the great mystic among the apostles, had much to tell the educated rabbinist of Tarsus, schooled in the Law and the tradition, and in the best contemporary Judaism of Jerusalem. It was a meeting of the utmost importance, for it brought together the greatest mind and the greatest heart among the believers. Paul had indeed his great religious experiences; others had them too. But what marked him out in the Early Church was his power of thought.

So for two weeks these two greatest figures of the primitive church confessed, debated and conferred. Peter told again his unforgettable story of how he had denied his Lord, and Paul never forgot that he had been the persecutor of the church.

One of the things Paul learned from the Jerusalem believers was the oral gospel, that Aramaic summary of Jesus' ministry and teaching which primitive Christians gladly learned by heart, and taught new converts. Paul used to quote it in his letters, not as a written book, but as what he remembered from what earlier believers had told him. And in after years he would say to his converts, "I received from the Lord the account that I passed on to you," about the Last Supper and the death and Resurrection of Christ. This earliest form of the gospel story Paul put into Greek and taught his converts, everywhere, but no one troubled to write it down.

So Paul found Jerusalem a very different place from the Jerusalem he had known and lived in as a Pharisee and a persecutor. Then his associates were priests and rabbis, Pharisees and Sadducees. He had been acceptable to Gamaliel and the high priest. Now they know him no more. They think of him only as a renegade who has deserted the Jewish faith. His friends and intimates are the Nazarenes; in fact, he is one of them. Henceforth he fights on their side. The Jews' loss is the Christians' gain. Paul has brought them unexpected reinforcement. What a prodigious reinforcement it was to prove they could not have dreamed.

CHAPTER IV ❧ FINDING HIS TASK

PAUL WAS going home. His visit to Peter at Jerusalem lasted only a fortnight. He spent two weeks with him and then left for Syria and Cilicia.[1] After years of absence, he was returning to Tarsus. He must have done so with grave misgivings, for he was a changed man, and his reception there was sure to be a painful one. To his people, his parents if they were still living, he seemed to have abandoned all they held most dear. One wonders whether they even received him at all, under the circumstances. Paul was certainly not the man to have withheld the bold statement of his new faith. If they had followed him into the Christian circle, the fact would almost certainly have been reflected in The Acts or in his letters. He spent some years in Tarsus but hardly under his father's roof. Jesus had said that whoever loved father or mother more than him was not worthy of him, and Paul, we may be sure, did no such thing. His trade gave him a living, and he had an opportunity to learn the great lesson he afterwards passed on to the Philippians, of being contented with any condition in which he found himself. With his daily work he probably found opportunity to declare his views in the local synagogue and gained some adherents there, as well as in other Cilician towns.

Meantime, events were marching rapidly in other Jewish centers. The persecution of the believers in Jerusalem, precipitated by the case of Stephen, had led many to leave Jerusalem and take refuge wherever they could. Some had found their way to Phœnicia, some to the island of Cyprus and some to Antioch. Everywhere they went they preached, privately at least, but only to Jews or converts to Judaism. But at length in Antioch some Greek-speaking Jews from Cyprus and the North African city of Cyrene began to preach directly to Greeks with no Jewish background. These were people whose previous religious connections had been with the ethnic faith of older Greek religion, or with the philosophical faiths of Stoicism or Epicureanism, or with the mystery religions, with their dying and rising hero-deities, their initiation mysteries and their common religious meals. They found that even these heathen could be reached and attracted to faith in Christ; in fact, these people began to come into the Christian circle in such numbers that the leaders down in Jerusalem learned of it and despatched Paul's old friend Barnabas to the scene, more than three hundred miles away. So fast and far the new cause was spreading and taking root. With all their other endowments, its leaders in Jerusalem were wide-awake, energetic men, swift to recognize and follow its advance.

Barnabas was a Levite from Cyprus, and a man of understanding and judgment. His name was Joseph, but the apostles had named him Barnabas, "Son of Encouragement." He was probably at home in Antioch, since he came from the near-by island of Cyprus. His Greek background would help him to understand this new work among Greeks at Antioch. He was also a man of impressive appearance, for the people of Lystra afterwards took him for Zeus, when they called his companion, Paul, Hermes. We can picture him as an august, bearded figure, benign and dignified.

Barnabas was delighted with the new work among the Greeks at Antioch and threw himself into it with great energy. He must have been a man of great breadth and liberality, to be so ready to welcome this host of Greek believers into the Christian fellowship, which had previously been accessible only to those who had had some Jewish connection. Even Cornelius of Cæsarea had been an adherent of Judaism, a God-fearing man, though not actually a proselyte. But now at Antioch the gospel is offered directly to Greeks, with no previous Jewish connection, however slight, and their response was surprising. A considerable number of them joined the church at Antioch.

The new work was so successful and exacting that Barnabas was led to a momentous decision, destined to have consequences greater than he can have dreamed. He needed help and looked about for a man to give it, and he thought of Paul, the converted Pharisee, now in a sort of retirement in the neighboring city of Tarsus. Christians and Christian groups were evidently in frequent communication with one another. Tarsus was only eighty miles away in a straight line, but much farther as Barnabas traveled. He went over to Tarsus himself to find Paul and prevail upon him to come back to Antioch and take up this new work among the Greeks there with him. Paul welcomed the opportunity. He had now been in Tarsus for eight or ten years, doubtless steadily at work preaching the gospel to all whom he could reach. They must have been mostly Greeks rather than Jews, for the synagogue there must soon have disowned his efforts. It may well have been in these lonely years of struggle in Tarsus that Paul experienced another of those synagogue beatings with forty lashes less one of which he afterwards wrote to the Corinthians. They must have been hard and bitter years, with his old friends arrayed against him at every turn.

These are the most obscure years in Paul's Christian life, but they formed an important period of reflection, adjustment and preparation. In them he was developing the realization of the values of the Christian experience that was to mark all his later work, and learning how to approach Greeks with the gospel.

News of Paul's work in Tarsus among the Greeks there and of his deep concern for such work among the heathen had evidently reached Barnabas at Antioch. The conviction had long been formed in Paul's mind that it was God's will that he should preach the gospel to the heathen. Even at the time of his conversion, back in Damascus, Ananias had had a vision that Paul was to carry the gospel to heathen as well as Jews, and when he went back to Jerusalem, Paul himself praying one day in the Temple felt divinely assured that God wished him to carry the gospel to the heathen. He was by this time an experienced preacher to the Greek public. The invitation of Barnabas offered him a golden opportunity to carry on what he felt to be his special mission in one of the great Greek centers of the ancient world, the neighboring city of Antioch.

However many Jews there were in Antioch, it was preeminently a heathen city, where Greek and Oriental paganisms mingled in a sensual and degrading worship.

Daphne, the pleasure ground of the city, was notorious for its vices, and the city had become a synonym for pleasure-seeking immorality. When Juvenal wished to describe the depravity of Rome, he said the Orontes had emptied into the Tiber. Still, Antioch the beautiful was rated the third city in the empire, surpassed only by Rome and Alexandria, and Paul could not have asked a finer field for the mission to the heathen to which he felt called. He returned with Barnabas to Antioch. There they worked together for a year, preaching and reasoning with the varied Greek population. They probably still maintained a foothold in the synagogues, but the work among the non-Jewish people in Antioch assumed such proportions that the disciples could no longer be described as a new Jewish sect, and they came to be called Christians there. This was a word of Latin formation, meaning partisans of Christ, members of his party, or even slaves or soldiers of his, like Herodians in Palestine. Being just a popular nickname, it was probably not welcomed by the disciples. It is little used in the New Testament [2] and sparingly in other Christians' writings before A.D. 150.

Paul no doubt found work at his trade in the busy bazaars of Antioch, for it was against his principles to accept money for preaching, a point on which he and the Corinthians afterwards so sharply differed. The ancient working day was a very long one, but what little leisure remained at the end of it and his weekly day off he would devote to preaching in the synagogue or, like the Stoic preachers, in the street, very much after the Salvation Army pattern today. Nor did he fail to improve the opportunities for presenting the gospel offered by his shop or the casual social contacts of a great bustling city.

So began the Greek mission, which was so soon to become the main stream of Christian advance. Much has been made of the spread of the Greek language over the eastern part of the empire even to Rome itself, as a preparation for Christianity. But even more significant and providential was the spread of Greek culture, the work of the dramatists grappling with great problems of duty and destiny, and the great philosophers, especially the religious ones, like Socrates, Plato, and in Luke's own lifetime, Epictetus. While the Romans still thronged the amphitheaters and found enjoyment in seeing gladiators fight wild beasts to the death, the Greeks went to the theater and saw great plays by Aeschylus, Sophocles or Euripedes, or to the gymnasium and the stadium, to take part in their characteristic athletic sports, some of which are reflected in the figures Paul used in his letters. They were as a class much more cultivated than the Romans and more ready for the spiritual message of the new faith.

The movements of Paul and of Barnabas in traveling about Palestine and the adjacent lands cause us some surprise, when we think of the difficulties of ancient travel, even in those Roman times, when roads and bridges built by the Romans had done much to facilitate it. This extraordinary capacity for travel was one of the characteristics of Paul, who was to a remarkable degree a citizen of the world in which he lived. No pent-up Utica confined his powers. He was a man of world horizons, as his journeys and, still more, his letters show.

Among the travelers who came to Antioch in the days when Saul and Barnabas were so busy there were some Christian prophets from Jerusalem and one of them foretold a famine which was to prevail all over the world. And just as the Jews out in the Greek world took it upon themselves to supply the needs of their poor Jewish brethren in Jerusalem, so now the Christians of these great Greek cities began to look after their Christian brethren there. A collection was taken to be sent to the authorities in Jerusalem, and Barnabas carried it down to that city.[3]

Years after, when the Jerusalem leaders urged Paul and his associates to remember the Christian poor of Jerusalem, as Paul tells us in Galatians, he felt that this was something he had already taken pains to do, probably remembering his efforts to raise money at Antioch in his first ministry there, for Jerusalem relief. This humane practical interest marked Paul's work from beginning to end, for it was another such relief enterprise for Jerusalem that long after cost him his liberty and eventually his life.

Barnabas returned from his relief visit to Jerusalem with a new recruit for the missionary enterprise, his youthful cousin John, who was called Mark, and who was evidently a promising member of the Jerusalem church destined for a varied and important rôle in the unfolding drama of the Greek mission. He was probably a young man in his early twenties when Barnabas brought him to Antioch.

Mark is a most interesting, human, influential and yet mysterious figure in primitive Christianity, for he did more to shape Christian memories of the life and work of Jesus than any other man of his generation, and yet we know almost nothing about him. It was like those founders to disappear behind their work. For one thing, he has a Jewish name, John, and a Latin name, Marcus, which we Anglicize as Mark. The house of his mother Mary in Jerusalem was a recognized rallying place for the disciples; Peter went to it when he was released from prison. Mark's cousin Barnabas was, as we have seen, a man of some property and came from Cyprus. The family thus had a foothold in the Greek world as well as in Jerusalem. Mark was to enjoy the unique distinction of close association with Paul and then Peter, whose interpreter and reporter he finally became, with consequences of the utmost significance, for many years later, in Rome after Peter's death, he assembled his memories of Peter's memorabilia of Jesus into what we know as the Gospel of Mark.[4] But that was twenty-five years after his coming to Antioch and his association with Barnabas and Saul there. All in all, Mark's Christian career is one of the most varied and instructive that we know of, and in his own field he performed a service of the highest significance to the Christian cause, as the writer of its first book, and the creator of the gospel type of literature. It was no ordinary assistant that Barnabas brought back with him to Antioch.

Barnabas was clearly a man who saw possibilities in individuals about him and brought them forward, giving them opportunities to show what they could do. He had certainly done this for Paul, and he now did it for his Jerusalem cousin Mark. His own services to the Christian cause were great, but small in comparison with the accomplishments of these two men who began their work at least as his protégés. We can begin to understand why the apostles had named him the "Son of Encouragement."

The absence of Barnabas on this relief visit to Jerusalem left Paul in charge of their great work among the Greeks in Antioch; for the time being he was at its head. Antioch has been called the first fulcrum of Christianity. It was there that the disciples began to be called Christians. They had ceased to be a sect of Judaism. The movement was coming to self-consciousness and finding new breadth and vision in the great Greek city on the Orontes. For the little while that Paul was in command of the Greek mission there, he was finding his first opportunity to try out his capacity for leadership. That great reconstruction of his inner world which had begun in Damascus and continued in Arabia and Tarsus was still going on. No more important thinking was being done anywhere in the world than Paul was doing as he preached and pondered and debated among the Greeks of Antioch. Perhaps he was beginning to be conscious of the extraordinary powers he was to show when he carried the gospel on to the shores of Europe and opened a new continent to the Christian cause. Certainly at Tarsus and Antioch Paul became convinced of his vocation; his mission was to the heathen, the Greeks of the Roman west. He had found his task.

CHAPTER V ❧ PENETRATING THE GREEK WORLD

A REMARKABLE group of men was now gathered in the church at Antioch. Prophets and teachers, they included Barnabas of Cyprus, Symeon called Niger, Lucius of Cyrene, Manaen, who had been an intimate friend of the tetrarch Herod Antipas, and Saul of Tarsus. Mark was there too, but he was as yet too young and inexperienced to be listed with these five. They were men of great faith and wide vision. The new work among the Greeks which had begun in Antioch and its surprising success had opened their eyes to still larger possibilities, and with a profound sense of divine guidance they ordained Barnabas and Paul to go out into the Greek world as missionaries. So Antioch became the first missionary church, and the Greek mission was begun. Great consequences hung upon this decision, for in half a century Christianity was to become a Greek movement.

The first great step had been the preaching to the Greeks in Antioch. Who took that step we do not know. But Barnabas soon came on from Jerusalem to superintend its consequences, and soon after Paul was brought over from Tarsus to help in the new movement. Now it assumes the offensive. It begins to invade the neighboring Greek centers. As the two missionaries set out, they take Mark with them as their assistant. In this capacity he probably made arrangements for their travel and entertainment, like a dragoman or courier today; the Greek word means servant. But he would also help in their religious work, very much as Timothy helped Paul in his later journeys. It was an apprenticeship in Christian missionary service; today we would call him a secretary.

A great sense of divine guidance pervaded the missionaries and the church at Antioch which had sent them out. This consciousness of the Spirit of Christ, which was the Spirit of God, the Holy Spirit, colored and controlled all their actions. This was in fact the preëminent attitude and experience of these primitive believers.

The first objective of the missionary party was Barnabas' native land, the island of Cyprus. As a former resident of the island, Barnabas knew conditions there and probably still had a foothold somewhere on the island—friends, relatives, perhaps his old home, certainly his old synagogue. Barnabas is the leader of the expedition; it is Barnabas and Saul, not yet "Paul and Barnabas." It was Jews from Cyprus who had first preached the gospel to Greeks in Antioch, and others there might favor such a movement. They sailed from Seleucia, the port of Antioch, sixteen miles from that metropolis, and came to the town of Salamis, a distance of one hundred and thirty miles in a straight line from Seleucia. Cyprus was only sixty miles off the Syrian coast, and communication was frequent.

The missionaries began their preaching in the Jewish synagogues of Salamis, where their zeal and eloquence made them welcome guests. Great numbers of Jews had made their homes in Cyprus. It was the third largest island in the Mediterranean, famous for its fertility, its deposits of copper, which took its name from Cyprus, and its worship of the Cyprian Venus, Aphrodite, the Astarte of the Phœnicians. It was from her famous shrine there in Paphos, the capital of Cyprus, that her worship, anciently derived from Phœnicia, had spread among the Greeks.

What route the missionaries followed in Cyprus we cannot certainly say; there were roads along the north and south coasts, with towns along the south coast every twenty or twenty-five miles; but also through the east-west plain, the Mesaoria, which stretched westward from Salamis, the principal town of the island, where they landed, to Soli, on its western side.

This last was probably the course the missionaries took. It is still the usual way to get from one end of the island (Famagusta, near the site of Salamis) through the Mesaoria, the plain that forms the interior of Cyprus, to Soli at the western end. From there they would follow the coast road around to Paphos. It is at Soli that American engineers have rediscovered and reopened the ancient mines which gave the Greco-Roman world its chief supplies of copper.

Barnabas and Paul certainly visited Paphos, for there they reached the proconsul, Sergius Paulus. He heard of their preaching and invited them to tell him their message. Like many officials of antiquity—Babylonian, Persian, Greek, Roman, and even of today—he had a magician or astrologer in his court, and this man, jealous of his own prestige, tried to silence the missionaries. From an Old Testament point of view he would, of course, be rated a "false prophet," since prophecy was one of the rôles of such astrologers. It was then that Saul, who like the proconsul was a Paulus, denounced the astrologer with crushing effect, and the proconsul was convinced and believed. An inscription found at Soli, dated in A.D. 52–53, records his name, Paulus, and mentions him as a recent governor.[1] From this time on, The Acts speaks of Saul no longer by his Hebrew name but by his Roman, probably because he was now turning more and more in his missionary work to a Greco-Roman public. And from now on Paul replaces Barnabas as the leader of the little group. It is no longer Barnabas and Saul, but Paul and his companions, or Paul and Barnabas. In more ways than one, the contact with the Cyprus proconsul changes Paul's position in the eyes of his companions and probably in his own eyes also. From now on, certainly, he travels, preaches and writes no longer as a Jew but as a member of the empire. Since his experience at Damascus, Paul had given up a great deal of his social and spiritual inheritance in Judaism. He seems now to sever the last tie, when he relinquishes his Jewish name. That it was he who did this, and not just his historian in writing about him, is clear from his letters, in which he always names himself as "Paulus," Paul.

At Paphos the missionaries left Cyprus. Barnabas and Mark returned to it later, on their Second Missionary Journey, but Paul did not go there again. It was as if he assigned it to Barnabas as his responsibility. The Sergius Paulus incident, however, remained in his mind, and no wonder, for it was his first successful contact with the Roman authorities. This proconsul was no palace freedman like Felix, but a genuine Roman patrician.

How few ancient travelers we can follow about on a map

as we can Paul! From Paphos the party sailed directly to Pamphylia, a small province in the middle of the south coast of Asia Minor. They landed at Perga, which was not on the sea but a few miles up the River Cestrus. It was the principal city of Pamphylia, and its remains today are probably more complete than those of any other city Paul visited. For Perga, we are told, looks like a place inhabited or only just abandoned. On the acropolis for a length of almost a thousand yards and a depth of six hundred and fifty, battlemented walls stand perfect, with turrets seventy paces square, in many cases as high as when first built. The streets cross at right angles; from the southern gate a street flanked with columned halls leads up to the center of the citadel; the theater and stadium could seat about eleven thousand spectators. This may well have been the aspect of the city when Paul landed there.

The missionaries seem to have gone there intending to preach in Pamphylia. It would be the next land to be evangelized, lying next to Cilicia, where Paul had already preached in Tarsus. But they did little or no missionary work there. Just what happened in Perga is a good deal of a mystery. For one thing, Mark left them and went home to Jerusalem; for another, Paul and Barnabas went straight up out of the low-lying coastland to the highlands of Galatia, probably to get relief from the pestilential climate of the coast. Some years later Paul reminded the Galatians that it was because of illness that he had first preached the gospel to them. Soon after arriving at Perga, he must have been overtaken by the malaria that haunts the shores of Asia Minor; Mark had become disheartened, and perhaps sick;

he may have urged the older men that they all return to Antioch. At any rate, he abandoned the expedition and went home, in circumstances which made Paul lose faith in him as a missionary companion and refuse to take him on later missionary journeys. It is easy to understand this, if Paul was taken ill at Perga and Mark chose that moment to withdraw from the party and sail for home. Paul might well think he was a young man one could not depend on in a crisis. But Barnabas stood by his young cousin and made him his companion on a later journey to Cyprus.

Antioch lay about a hundred miles due north from Perga, at an elevation of about thirty-nine hundred feet above the sea. It was finely situated and offered some prospect of relief from the malarial coastland. The road probably followed the valley of the Cestrus for some distance, but it must have been a trying journey for a sick man. Paul's words to the Galatians show that he was far from well when he arrived among them: "What must have tried you in my physical condition, you did not scorn and despise, but you welcomed me like an angel of God, like Christ Jesus himself." As malarial fever was often regarded as a punishment sent by God, this attitude of the Galatians toward Paul's illness was the more remarkable.

In a terrific list of the hardships and perils he had undergone in the Christian cause, Paul afterwards wrote the Corinthians of many such experiences for which we can find no definite place in his travels. He speaks of his frequent journeys, with their danger from rivers, danger from robbers, toil and hardship, "through many a sleepless night, through hunger and thirst, often without food and exposed to cold," and memories of this sudden journey into the mountains of Asia Minor may have been in his mind. It was a climb of almost four thousand feet above sea level, through a robber-infested region on a road or trail of much more than a hundred miles, that wound uphill all the way, except where it forded mountain torrents or surmounted passes in the Taurus. It must have taken between one and two weeks, and if Paul's state of health is what we have supposed, we can hardly think he made this difficult journey on foot. For no safe, well-paved and well-traveled Roman highway led north from Perga to Antioch. The missionaries had to find their way over mountain trails from the valley of the Cestrus, we may suppose, into that of the Eurymedon and so into the fertile and hospitable plain where Antioch stood. We can hardly realize the casual character of ancient travel, especially in out-of-the-way parts of Asia Minor. In them there were no stages or busses, no caravans to which one might attach oneself for security and company if nightfall found the traveler far from town or shelter. But once Antioch was reached, this situation was changed, for it lay on the great caravan route that traversed the length of Asia Minor all the way from Syria to Ephesus.

So Paul and Barnabas found themselves in the heart of Asia Minor in the city of Antioch "toward Pisidia," for it was not really in that little country, but only near it. It was one of the sixteen cities Seleucus Nicator had founded and named for his father Antiochus, who had been one of the generals of Philip of Macedon, the father of Alexander. Roman reorganization seventy years before Paul's visit had begun to Romanize the old Greek city, which had long contained a substantial Jewish element in its population, and it was now a part of the Roman province of Galatia. It lay on what its people called the "olive-clad Anthian plain," where the great highway across the highlands of Asia Minor swung north to get around the large double lake which the people called Limnae—the Lakes—beyond which it went on to Apollonia and Apamea, on its way to the Greek cities on the Ægean. Antioch lay only a few miles from these mountain lakes high in the Taurus range. It was one of the thriving, busy cities of the uplands of Anatolia.

The Sabbath found the missionaries in the Jewish synagogue sharing in its chants and prayers. They must have made a favorable impression, for they were invited to speak to the congregation. Now it was Paul who responded, assuring them that their Messiah had at last come in the person of Jesus and offered them a forgiveness and reconciliation beyond anything the Law could afford. This bold presentation was received with a good deal of favor; many of the Jews went with Paul and Barnabas to talk further about it, and they were invited to come again the next Sabbath and repeat what they had said. When they appeared to do so, a great crowd was assembled; it seemed as if the whole town was gathered to hear them. Paul himself wrote the Galatians afterwards: "I can bear witness that you would have torn out your very eyes, if you could, and given them to me!" After his disheartening experience at Perga, this was an auspicious opening of what was to be his first great mission, the mission to the Galatians.

CHAPTER VI ❧ LEADERSHIP IN GALATIA

THE MARKED success that Paul and Barnabas had so quickly met with in their preaching in the synagogue at Antioch aroused the envy and animosity of their Jewish hosts, who contradicted what the missionaries said and condemned them for saying it. Paul and Barnabas replied that the Christian message had first to be offered to Jews but since they refused it, they would turn to the heathen and offer it to them, for such were their instructions; God had made them a light for the heathen to be the means of salvation to the very ends of the earth. This ancient commission of the Servant of Jehovah the missionaries now claimed as their authority for preaching the new gospel directly to the heathen peoples of Galatia. These non-Jewish groups accepted the new faith with enthusiasm, and the movement was spreading fast when an agitation stirred up against Paul and Barnabas forced them to leave Antioch for a while. This was brought about through well-to-do women of Jewish religious inclinations as well as through the leading men of the town, who probably saw in the matter one of those race conflicts which were and are so likely to end by disturbing the peace. At all events the Jews denounced Paul and Barnabas to these prominent Greek residents so vehemently that they forced them to leave Antioch.

Paul and Barnabas knew when to give ground and when

to press their advantage. The experiment of preaching the gospel to the heathen, which had done so well in Antioch in Syria, had done equally well here in another Antioch in the very heart of Asia Minor. They left Antioch, but only to go eighty or ninety miles eastward along the Roman road to the town of Iconium. It was a thickly settled region through which they now traveled, with towns every twenty miles or so, but Iconium was distinguished in Lycaonia for its favorable situation, for a river refreshed the arid plain and had from the most ancient times marked the spot for a city.

The old Oriental Phrygian town had been rebuilt and reorganized by the Greek genius after Alexander, and more recently the Romans, too, had shown it marked encouragement, letting it and the neighboring towns of Laodicea and Derbe compound the name of the emperor Claudius with theirs, into Claud-Iconium, Claudio-Derbe and Claudio-Laodicea. Beside these Oriental, Greek and Roman forces, there were Jews in Iconium, and, although Paul and Barnabas had ostensibly turned to the heathen with their message, they again as often after began with the synagogue. The success of their preaching there led to further clashes with the Jews and finally to threats of mob violence. Warned that they were likely to be set upon and stoned, Paul and Barnabas made their escape from Iconium and made their way southward six hours' journey to the town of Lystra, which enjoyed the dignity of being styled a Roman colony, like Antioch, though a place of much less importance. Here conditions were unlike those in Antioch and Iconium. We hear of no synagogue to preach in, and the populace still speaks the old Lycaonian tongue, along with the more fashionable Greek language. The cure of a lame man rouses the people to frenzy, and they hail the missionaries as gods, identifying Barnabas as Zeus and Paul as Hermes, because he did most of the speaking. They were even on the point of offering sacrifices to them when the missionaries, learning of the plan, had the greatest difficulty in putting a stop to it. The story recalls the old Phrygian legend of the appearance of Zeus and Hermes to a hospitable couple, Philemon and Baucis, which forty years before Ovid had immortalized in his *Metamorphoses*.

The incident gives us one of our few hints as to what Paul looked like. He was evidently much younger than Barnabas, and the comparison with Hermes suggests a graceful and attractive figure of young manhood. What the Corinthians a few years later said of his personal appearance as insignificant was spoken not judicially but in malice and anger, and probably meant no more than that Paul did not look like a Plato or a Moses. Hermes was the symbol of gracious youth; the Hermes of Praxiteles at Olympia is the proof of that. And Luke evidently liked to remember Paul as such a figure.

Whatever degree of preaching directly to the heathen had been achieved at Antioch in Syria, or in Cyprus, or in Antioch and Iconium in Galatia, in Lystra there was nothing else to do; there were no synagogues to start from, and no Jews to speak of. Yet here a group of believers was formed, and things were going smoothly when Jews from Antioch and Iconium, who had not lost sight of the missionaries' movements, made their appearance in Lystra and stirred up an attack on Paul, which nearly cost him his life. He was stoned and dragged out of the city for dead. The Christian disciples rallied around him, and he recovered sufficiently to get up and go back with them into the town. Great determination was matched in Paul with great physical endurance. Perhaps the memory of what he had done to Stephen steeled him to face any physical violence that might come. He had almost gone the way he had sent Stephen. It was his only experience of this sort; as he wrote to the Corinthians afterwards, in the catalog of his hardships and perils in the missionary cause, "I have been stoned once." Stoning was no playful matter, such as the mudslinging one may experience in a modern Moslem town like Hebron. It was grim, deadly business—a Jewish form of execution. Even Paul with all his beatings had been stoned only once, and once was ordinarily enough; it was usually fatal. But the next day he went on, as he had gone on under sharp pressure from Antioch and again from Iconium, now from Lystra, and makes his way to a new refuge, in the partly Romanized town of Derbe, forty miles from Lystra by the Roman road, the Via Augusta, built under Augustus a generation before.

Claudio-Derbe was a little Lycaonian city, half Greek and half Oriental, but even here a group of believers was formed by the determined missionaries. And Derbe became in more ways than one a turning point in their work. They had come to it as a refuge from hostility in Lystra, and secondarily as a field for their mission work. In Derbe they seem to have been unmolested. Their enemies in

Antioch and Iconium were prepared to pursue them one day's journey, to Lystra, but that was far enough. They did not renew the chase for a second day's journey. Paul and Barnabas had escaped and were safe.

Ever since reaching the healthful uplands of Antioch near Pisidia and their short stay there, Paul and Barnabas had been moving east and south, in the general direction of Tarsus and Antioch in Syria, their headquarters. By the Roman roads they were perhaps one-third of the way home from Antioch near Pisidia to Antioch in Syria. The natural thing to do was to go on—on to Laranda, and then either by Tyana, as Xenophon and the Ten Thousand had done, in 401 B.C., or by a lower route over to the Cilician Gates, the famous pass over the Taurus, down to Tarsus, and then on eastward to Antioch. Paul and Barnabas had done a noble piece of evangelism in the face of bitter opposition and might well leave its resumption to a later time. They had gone over the ground in Cyprus only once, though there they had developed no serious antagonism. Moreover, they had had serious setbacks. Paul had been very sick, doubtless with the prevailing malaria; they had lost the help of Mark, and they had had a very rough journey up to Antioch. They might well return to Antioch in Syria and wait for more favorable conditions in Galatia.

Yet there is no hint in the story in The Acts that the two missionaries ever even thought of such a thing. They were simply biding their time in Derbe, planning to renew the attack all along the line, in each of the danger points, waiting either for things to cool down, as we say, or perhaps for the turn of the official year to bring about a change of government in the Greek city states, which would give them a chance for a fresh hearing. What Paul says in Galatians makes it plain that the people in these cities who had listened to their message had given them such a welcome that they could not leave them unorganized and unstabilized. A few weeks' work among them now would mean far more than it could a year or two later. At Derbe, Paul and Barnabas make the momentous decision to return to the three cities from which they had barely escaped with their lives and try to put their work in them on a permanent basis.

This was a step not only of great practical sagacity but of no little personal heroism. The New Testament narratives never pause to praise their heroes for their courage; they simply take it for granted. Such reticence must not blind us to the bravery of these two men in turning their backs on an honorable return to Antioch to face once more the hostile groups that had just driven them from one city and then another and pursued them to a third with actual violence and imminent death. Yet back they went to Lystra, Iconium and Antioch, to reassemble their followers in each place and take some steps toward church organization.[1] It was this revisiting of these places that made the work in them permanent, so that one could say there were really churches in Galatia. Then down the Taurus steeps again to the coast—Perga, where they could now preach, as they evidently had not done before, and then the port of Attalia, where they could take ship for Antioch.

It was a historic moment when before the assembled church of Antioch Paul and Barnabas made their report on this first Christian missionary journey, and the chief point in their story was that out in the provinces of the empire the heathen had welcomed and accepted their message. Their experience in Antioch did not stand alone; Greeks in Cyprus and in the heart of Asia Minor, three hundred miles away, had felt the voice of God in their message and had responded to it.

The First Missionary Journey was an enterprise of the utmost importance in Christian history. Yet the Jews were no strangers to the missionary impulse.[2] From the time of Alexander, religion about the eastern Mediterranean had been coming to be less an inheritance than a personal experience. The mystery religions and the philosophic faiths had been winning adherents from various nations and had done much to accustom the ancients to the idea of internationalism in religion; they no longer simply grew up in the faith of their fathers. Religion was an individual and personal matter. Judaism, too, had been making its appeal for understanding and acceptance; much of the Apocrypha literature reflects this desire for a better appreciation of Judaism on the part of the Greeks. The translation of the Hebrew Scriptures into Greek—the Septuagint Version— was due to this desire. The writings of Philo and Josephus and the Sibylline Oracles in the first and second centuries are not only apologetic, defending Judaism, but propagandist, seeking to spread it among Greek readers. Certainly later on Jewish messengers—"apostles"—were sent out from time to time from Jewish centers to instruct, correct, and collect funds. Saul's mission to Damascus for the high priest is an instance. Proselytes were certainly welcomed to the Jewish fold. The Gospel of Matthew says of the Pharisees that they scoured sea and land to make one convert. Matthew was probably written in Antioch, and this saying may reflect Jewish attitudes there.

That the Jews ever organized expeditions for propagandist purposes we have no clear evidence. What Barnabas and Saul had done was more like the procedure of the wandering Stoic preachers, yet even they seem to have done nothing so purposeful and systematic. In short, it was something very bold and novel in religious work that Barnabas and Saul had begun in this missionary tour, which we know so well that we take it quite for granted. Christianity was indeed spreading fast by casual contacts: by Philip riding for a few hours with a pilgrim from Ethiopia who was traveling in the same direction; by personal contacts on ships or at inns, on business or pleasure—these were some of the ways in which this great new experience in religion was being communicated from person to person.

But Barnabas and Saul are not traveling for business or pleasure. They are traveling to carry the gospel to distant places and to carry it to Greeks—people not already attached to the Jewish faith. These are the things that make their First Missionary Journey significant and even momentous. Its results encouraged both of them to repeat it later. Certainly for Paul it became an accepted method of religious work. It was an experiment in Christian promotion and for all its hardships and dangers they counted it a success.

CHAPTER VII 🙣 AN INTERNATIONAL RELIGION

THE RETURN of Paul and Barnabas to Antioch from this remarkable journey was followed by a no less remarkable meeting at Jerusalem, the first of the kind in the history of Christianity, and one of the most momentous. On their return the missionaries settled down again to their work among the vast non-Jewish population of the city and were once more absorbed in it when some Jewish visitors arrived from Judea and began to circulate the idea that these believers from the Greek world must accept circumcision and virtually become Jews if they were to be saved. This was far from the view held by Paul and Barnabas, and taught by them to their Greek converts in Antioch, Cyprus and Galatia. If it was permitted to go unchallenged, all their work would be undone, and their converts left in confusion and dismay. The matter must be laid before the leaders of the church at Jerusalem; and who could present the Greek side so well as Paul and Barnabas?

Almost fourteen years had passed since Paul's last visit to Jerusalem, when he had his interviews with Cephas. He felt an inner voice directing him to go, and no doubt the church at Antioch, disturbed by the work of the men from Judea, endorsed his going and sent Barnabas with him. There were at least three in the delegation, for Paul took with him a Greek convert named Titus, probably as a living example of the kind of believer about whom the controversy had arisen. This man was afterwards of the greatest use to Paul in his correspondence with the Corinthian Christians, but he is never mentioned in The Acts, which has led some to the fanciful but attractive view that he was Luke's brother. Paul speaks of Titus and "his brother" in II Corinthians: "I am sending with him his brother, who is famous in all the churches for his work in spreading the good news." Certainly the man who could afterwards write the Gospel of Luke and the book of Acts must have been an eloquent preacher.

Paul laid the question of the freedom of Gentile converts from accepting circumcision and the rest of the Jewish Law before the recognized leaders of the church in Jerusalem, James the brother of Jesus, Cephas (Peter), and John, the surviving son of Zebedee, since John's brother James had been killed by Herod Agrippa five or six years before, about A.D. 42 or 43.

Paul felt profoundly that Christian faith must not be cramped and hampered by any entanglement with the Jewish Law. He himself had escaped from its toils only after an agonizing experience, and he was unalterably convinced that it could have no place at all in the Christian life. His success in winning Greeks out in the Roman west to faith in Christ as evidenced by the case of Titus, showed that the Law was altogether unnecessary to the experience of faith in Christ, and Paul was satisfied that it could only hamper and hinder it. Moreover, to require circumcision of Greek converts would of itself make the Christian movement just another sect of Judaism and reduce it to a subordinate part of what was essentially a national religion. But Paul saw in Christ far more than the Messiah of Jewish expectation; he saw in him a Savior for all mankind, Greek as well as Jew. In fact, as Paul viewed it, Jews had no more right or privilege in the religion he was preaching than Greeks or barbarians. No nation's people had any advantage or priority in it. It was for men and women, slaves and freemen, Greeks and Jews alike. The demands of the Judaizing visitors from Jerusalem had precipitated a question of tremendous scope and of the utmost importance. The whole character of the Christian Church hung on the issue.

This conception of Christian faith had much in common with some things the prophets had said long before; they had spoken boldly for the inwardness of religion and declared ceremonial and sacrifice matters of complete indifference. But the nation's religious life had taken the other course, and the position so boldly taken by the prophets was far from the attitude characteristic of first-century Judaism, in which such views were completely submerged in demands for legalistic details and ceremonial observances. The Sadducees, who controlled the Temple, were the champions of the sacrifices, while the Pharisees insisted upon the minute observance of the Law and the ceremonial, which so effectively cut the Jewish people off from their fellow men. For one thing, it made it impossible for a Jew to eat with a Greek without incurring ceremonial defilement, and this of course gave deep offense to the Greeks, who very naturally felt that they were being looked down upon by the Jews as their inferiors, as was indeed the case. As Shakespeare's Shylock put it, "I will buy with you, sell with you, talk with you, walk with you, and so following; but I will not eat with you, drink with you, nor pray with you." [1]

In the house of some Jewish believer in Jerusalem, the three foremost men of the Jerusalem church met the delegation from Antioch—Paul, Barnabas and Titus—but confronted them with the group that was insisting that Greek converts accept some part at least of the Jewish Law, beginning with circumcision. This incensed Paul, who had evidently expected to lay his missionary story before the three "pillars" in a private conference; he regarded these Judaizers as false brothers, who had been smuggled in or had sneaked in as spies, scheming to destroy Christian freedom and reduce believers to slavery again. It is clear that he felt they had no business in the conference. No doubt Paul told the story of the missionary journey and its results in establishing churches out in the Greek world. He also declared his great doctrine of salvation by faith alone, over against the doctrine of salvation by law, the encroachments of which he so feared would destroy the Christian movement before it had fairly started.

We can hardly suppose that Paul's narrative of his missionary success, particularly in Galatia, was not interrupted again and again by the Judaizers present, while his doctrine of salvation by faith alone entirely apart from any obedience to the Law, must have filled them with horror and alarm. Religious views of such breadth seemed to them totally heretical, and their protest was so vehement that, reinforced as it was by tradition and practice, it almost carried the day. It took all Paul's power in argument, coupled with his tremendous conviction and his extraordinary missionary experience, to stem the tide, and it left in his mind a very sinister impression of his opponents, and their aims and methods.

Paul explained to the leaders of the Jerusalem church the gospel he had been preaching with such success at Antioch, in Cyprus and in Galatia, as a gospel of faith, that is an inward attitude of repentance, obedience and love to God, without any reference to the Jewish Law or any part of it. It was by this attitude alone, he maintained, that everyone, Jew or Greek, could attain uprightness and please God. This left no room for any part of the Jewish legal system, as such, and circumcision, the Sabbath, and the food regulations which made it impossible for Jews to eat with Gentiles without being ceremonially defiled, went by the board.

This was a prodigious step. It meant that the Jew had no advantage over the Greek in availing himself of the Christian salvation, though he had a great religious tradition behind him. But Paul persuaded the three leaders, Peter, James and John, that this course was the right one, and not even Titus, the Greek convert who had come to Jerusalem with him, was made to accept circumcision.

In Galatians Paul gives a spirited account of this scene. We see the three foremost leaders of the church in Jerusalem, James, Cephas and John, sitting almost as an informal court, with the ultra-Jewish or Judaizing group, whom Paul calls false brothers, representing the legalistic position, and Paul championing the freedom of Greek believers from any entanglement with the Jewish Law. Barnabas was no doubt present at Paul's side, but Paul was the fiery advocate of the freedom of the Greek believers. Titus too was present, and the "false brothers" demanded that he be circumcised. The three leaders did not think this necessary, but urged it upon Paul as a concession in the interests of harmony. But Paul was no appeaser; he would not hear of it, and he won his point. As he looked at it, such a concession would have dragged after it the whole miserable business of legalism and been fatal to Christian freedom and to Christian faith, since it would have seemed to combine the freedom of faith with bondage to the endless trivialities of legalism.

The leaders yielded to his demands. Titus did not have to be circumcised, and with that relaxation any obligation to fulfil the Law disappeared. James was Jesus' brother and Cephas and John were the survivors of the three of his apostles who had been closest to him. But what they had been made no difference to Paul. What mattered was the truth about the believer's relation to the Law. Nor did the great three contribute anything new to him. They recognized that he was commissioned to preach to the heathen, just as Peter was to preach to the Jews, that is, to carry on the Jewish mission, and they gave his work their approval, pledging their coöperation to him and Barnabas. They also expressed the hope that the missionaries to the heathen would continue to raise money for the poor believers in Jerusalem, for the Jewish residents there ever since the Exile certainly, as in modern times, had been dependent on their brethren in the commercial centers of the west for their living.

What an extraordinary thing it is that we possess an account of this scene, certainly one of the most momentous in all Christian history, from the hand of the chief participant! It plainly reflects the intensity of his feeling about the matter, and the great importance the question and the decision of it possessed for him. His severe characterization of his opponents—"false brothers smuggled in, who sneaked in to spy upon the freedom we enjoy in Christ Jesus, so as to reduce us to slavery again"—shows how great his concern over the whole matter was. Upon it, he saw, depended not simply the success of the Christian movement but the opening to mankind of a new era in religious experience and a new and closer approach to God. For the men who for their own selfish purposes were trying to obstruct and prevent this he had the bitterest words of condemnation. They were trying to effect a monopoly of the grace of God so that men would have to come to them to obtain it! What could really be more dreadful! And yet it is a claim that has been made again and again in the history of Christianity and is a constant peril even today. Yet how clear it is that any group that makes any such claim exposes itself to Paul's blasting condemnation, false brothers, smuggled and sneaking in, as spies upon Christian freedom, to make us slaves again. It was a time for strong, bold words, and Paul knew how to use them.

The decision at Jerusalem had been favorable to the Greek mission, and the matter was settled, but it did not remain so. Paul and his two companions went back to Antioch and resumed their work there. Some time later Cephas, as Paul liked to call Peter, visited Antioch, apparently for the first time, and entered heartily into the social life of the church there, eating with Greek Christians without scruple. But this fraternal fellowship was interrupted by the arrival of some other believers from Jerusalem, sent by James himself, evidently with some further instructions on the subject. These were very probably the ones mentioned in The Acts as resulting from the conference Paul and Barnabas had had with the three Jerusalem pillars, James, Cephas and John. But they were evidently promulgated only after Paul and Barnabas had left the scene, for Paul's account leaves no room even for such restrictions as they contain.

The requirements were that Greek believers must avoid what had been sacrificed to idols, the tasting of blood and of the meat of animals that had been strangled, and immorality. These are akin to the requirements anciently imposed by the Hebrews upon strangers living among them,[2] and would have the effect, as those regulations did, of reducing the Greek believers to a lower religious level than the Jewish ones occupied and thus introducing a class system into the church. In any case, they made Christian freedom not quite complete, and Paul was apprehensive of any reduction of it at all. Had he accepted them, we might all be getting our meat at kosher butcher shops to this day.

This explains the effect of the new arrivals upon Cephas and even upon Barnabas, for after the coming of these emissaries from James, Cephas retreated from his courageous companionship with the Greek believers and resumed his isolationist Jewish practices, or some of them; at any rate, he ceased to eat with heathen, that is, Greeks who had accepted the new faith. The other Jewish Christians were naturally influenced by the acknowledged head of the twelve apostles and followed his example, in defiance of their own inner convictions, and even Barnabas himself, Paul's comrade in the hardships of the missionary journey to the Greeks, went with them.

We can imagine the position in which Paul was left by this change in attitude. He stood forth as the champion of the full status of the Greek believers, on an equality with their Jewish brothers. If Barnabas, Cephas and the rest of the Jewish Christians in Antioch accepted the new ruling from James as to how believers from the heathen world must conduct themselves, Paul must have stood out as the sole intermediary, the one Jewish Christian who was prepared to admit Greek Christians to full standing in the church, without any rules or regulations whatever. For the moment certainly he stood alone. Paul's physical courage had been tested repeatedly, at Damascus where he was probably beaten by the Jews, and where he escaped by night over the wall; and again in Galatia, where he was stoned. Such hardships he was to go through again and again. But now it was his moral courage that was at stake. Would he for the sake of peace and the undisturbed prosecution of his work yield a little to his old associates and the acknowledged leaders of the churches, and consent to the very modest demands James was making?

No, he would not! For he saw all too clearly that the slightest concession to legalism gave up the whole principle for which he stood and which he saw was vital. For it was not so much a question of how much was required; it was a question of requirements as such. Any formal requirements borrowed from Judaism, any regimentation whatever, Paul perceived, betrayed a conviction that faith was not enough, but required supplementing. But Paul had arrived at the conclusion that faith was all-sufficient, and that legalistic observances simply revealed the Judaizers' doubts of its sufficiency.

In another historic scene, this time at Antioch, Paul took issue directly with Peter. We have the story in Paul's own words, written to the Galatians only three or four years later.

"But when Cephas came to Antioch, I opposed him to his face, for his own conduct condemned him. For until some people came from James, he used to eat with the heathen, but after they came, he began to draw back and hold aloof, for fear of the party of circumcision. The other Jewish Christians followed his example in concealing their real views, so that even Barnabas was carried away by their pose. But when I saw that they were not straightforward about the truth of the good news, I said to Cephas, right before them all, 'If you live like a heathen and not like a Jew, though you are a Jew yourself, why should you try to make the heathen live like Jews?' "

Paul goes on in Galatians to point out that Jews, who like himself had become Christians, had found salvation through faith in Christ and through nothing else, and he thought clearly enough to see that his former habits of cooking and eating had nothing whatever to do with it. In this of course he was in line with the great prophets of Israel who had so often declared that the ceremonial side of religion meant nothing in the sight of God.

> "For it is love I delight in, and not sacrifice;
> Knowledge of God, and not burnt offerings." [3]

> "Yet what does the Lord require of you,
> But to do justice, and to love kindness,
> And to walk humbly with your God?" [4]

Was Paul victorious at Antioch? This is one of the mysteries of primitive Christian history. He speaks to the Galatians as if he were. No doubt he thought he was. Certainly he succeeded in maintaining the liberty of the Greek Christians there from any bondage to the Law. Whether he succeeded also in convincing Peter and Barnabas to take his side against James and the Jerusalem church is more doubtful. Paul succeeded in silencing opposition in Antioch, and so considered the matter settled. But the Judaizers had not given up the battle, as later events were to prove.

CHAPTER VIII 🕭 CHRISTIANITY ENTERS EUROPE

A FEW MONTHS after the excitement over the attempted encroachments of the Judaizing brothers from Jerusalem, Paul proposed to Barnabas that they should revisit the churches they had established on their missionary journey and see how they were doing. He and Barnabas had already seen the value of revisiting newly established churches, when they turned back from Derbe to reinforce their work in Lystra, Iconium and Antioch. Perhaps the activity of the Judaizers in following them to Syrian Antioch in their efforts to control their teachings also inclined Paul to go back to Galatia to see how his Christian friends there were getting on.

Barnabas was ready enough to make the journey, and proposed to take his cousin Mark along, as they had done on the first journey. But this Paul declined to do. Mark's behavior in forsaking the missionary party at Perga on the first journey had made a deep impression on his mind, and he would not consent. The result was that he and Barnabas parted company, and divided the field, Barnabas and Mark taking Cyprus as their territory to revisit, and Paul taking Galatia.

But he did not wish to go alone, and found a congenial companion in one of the men who had brought James's regulations from Jerusalem to Antioch. Luke calls him Silas, but Paul always speaks of him by his Latin name,

Silvanus. He had been prominent in the life of the Jerusalem church and had followed the controversy over the treatment of Greek converts closely. James would hardly have made him one of the two bearers of his instructions to the church at Antioch if he had not been in sympathy with them, but Paul's arguments must have changed his views, or Paul would not have made him his colleague on his next missionary tour. He seems to have remained in Antioch after he and Judas Barsabbas had brought James's disturbing decrees there. If he had gone home to Jerusalem, Paul succeeded in bringing him back, to join his new expedition. Silvanus was a prophet, that is, a convincing preacher, and had all the courage Paul thought so indispensable for the missionary task. So it came about that he was associated with Paul in this momentous journey and that his name stands with Paul's at the head of our earliest Christian writings, the letters to the Thessalonians. For he shared with Paul the extraordinary achievement of carrying the Christian gospel out of Asia into Europe, where it was to find a new home.

Paul and Silvanus set out from Antioch, this time by land, visiting on their way such churches as were already springing up under the influence of Antioch. Their route lay northward from Antioch and twenty-five or thirty miles away crossed the Amanus range by the pass known as the Syrian Gates, through which Xenophon and the Ten Thousand had come four and a half centuries before on their way to take a hand in a Persian civil war. The missionaries' route followed the seacoast through the Syro-Cilician gates, a narrow pass between Mount Amanus and the sea, to Issus, in Cilicia, where Alexander, surprised and almost cut off by the Persian army in 334–333 B.C., had turned back to win one of his greatest victories. There may already have been a church (there was one later) at Alexandria Parva, officially called Alexandria opposite Issus, the town that Alexander founded in 333 B.C. to control the Syrian Gates. It gave rise to the modern Alexandretta. It was only forty or fifty miles from Antioch and must have been reached very early by local missionaries.

The distance from Issus to Paul's old home at Tarsus, Xenophon, who had covered it in the opposite direction in 401 B.C., had figured at thirty parasangs, about one hundred miles. The Ten Thousand made this distance in five stages, or days' marches, and Paul and Silas probably took about that length of time for it, though it involved the passage of two rivers, the Pyramus and the Sarus. Xenophon obligingly gives us the width of these rivers as six hundred and three hundred feet respectively. In this part of their journey, the missionaries were now and again on roads already made historic by the movements of Xenophon in 401 B.C. and of Alexander in 334 B.C., though both those Greek figures had been marching eastward.

At Tarsus, Paul's years of residence after his conversion must have produced a Christian group prepared to welcome him and his companion. From Tarsus their way led northward to the Cilician Gates, the famous pass over the Taurus Mountains. Xenophon made the distance of about seventy-five miles in four days' marches. He describes the pass as in his day a wagon road, extremely steep. Once over the mountains, and on the Anatolian highlands, Paul's route becomes more obscure. Did he still follow the main highway, which led northward to Adana, or Tyana, before turning eastward to find his way to his old friends in Derbe and Lystra? That was the way Xenophon and the Ten Thousand had come in 401 B.C. Or he may have followed the more direct but less traveled route from Podandus just beyond the pass, across by way of Cybistra and Laranda to Lystra. By either route the journey must have taken fully a week and been fraught with the perils of robbers already spoken of as characteristic of Anatolian travel.

Derbe had been the farthest point of the first journey, and from it Paul and Barnabas had turned back so courageously to face their foes and find their friends in the newly evangelized cities of Galatia. Now the missionaries found little to detain them in Derbe. The Galatians had welcomed Paul with great enthusiasm on his first visit and the Christians of Derbe must have given him and his companion Silas a hearty welcome.

At Lystra, too, Paul was no doubt warmly welcomed, among others by Timothy, a young man who had already joined the church there. Timothy was the son of a Jewish-Christian mother and a Greek father, and Paul saw in him the man he wanted for his secretary, or assistant, the post Mark had held for a short time in Cyprus. Timothy accepted the post, having first been circumcised, and thus established his Jewish status, so necessary if he was to join Paul in his approach to the synagogues. This conciliatory gesture to the Jewish groups Paul was mingling with in the Greek cities need not be thought an inconsistency on his part, after his fight in Jerusalem against the demand that Titus be circumcised. No one was demanding that Timothy be circumcised; Paul encouraged it, as a step likely to save embarrassment in his future work. Nor was Timothy a Gentile; he was half Jewish. Paul himself boldly said that he was prepared to be all things to all men, in his efforts to save them. Paul's plan of campaign was to enter a town and begin with the synagogue, going on from there to the Greek population. Timothy had not been compelled to accept circumcision in order to enter the church; that was the point at issue with the Judaizers. Certainly Paul found a valuable secretary in Timothy. His name stands with Paul's at the beginning of most of his extant letters, he went on errands of great importance for Paul in the Greek mission, and he was with him at the very end. Paul found in him the qualities he had felt were lacking in Mark, and Timothy was a strength and comfort to him all the rest of his life.

The revisiting of his churches brought Paul and his party again to Iconium, today one of the principal stops on the railway that winds through Asia Minor from Antioch to Istanbul. Antioch near Pisidia was also revisited. In all these places Paul's reception was cordial and hospitable in the extreme, as we know from what he said afterwards in Galatians of his relations with his Galatian converts. They overwhelmed him with their affection and devotion.

The missionaries next appear in Troas, on the shores of the Ægean, near the site of ancient Troy. But by what route they reached it from Antioch near Pisidia can only be conjectured. They were interested in preaching the gospel in the province of Asia, but the divine guidance which they so deeply felt discouraged the step. Their next idea was to enter Bithynia, the province directly north of Asia, but here again their inward monitor deterred them. To reach Troas they had to cross the province of Asia, and they probably set out over the mountains north of Antioch, and made their way in two days to Cayster Plain. For the next stage of their journey, Xenephon may serve as our guide, for he tells how the Ten Thousand covered the distance between Cayster Plain and Keramon Agora, a distance of a hundred miles, in three days' journey, the fastest rate ever achieved by the Ten Thousand, and certainly faster than Paul and his friends were likely to travel. Then as now, travelers on foot or on horseback would take four or five days for such a journey. The road westward led right on from Keramon Agora to Sardis, the old capital of Lydia, and a generation later the site of one of the seven churches of Asia. This was about a hundred miles, and from Sardis north and west to Troas would be a hundred and fifty miles more.

It was at Thyatira some forty miles north of Sardis and almost on the borders of Mysia that the road forked and the decision for or against Bithynia was probably made, for the eastern fork of the road led to that province, while the western one bore away by way of Pergamum through Mysia to Troas.

Paul was now in the neighborhood of the Ionian cities, that realm of legend and romance which rivaled Greece itself in its contribution to Hellenic literature and culture. Every city had a history of antiquity and distinction, and probably no province of the empire had so many famous cities in it as Asia. Almost every one of them—Ephesus, Colossæ, Laodicea, Hierapolis, Philadelphia, Sardis, Thyatira, Pergamum, Smyrna, Miletus—would within a generation become a seat of the new religion Paul was preaching. It was to prove marvelous soil for Christianity, which was to find a new capital in the great city of Ephesus. Yet Paul hesitated. Those inner voices bade him look farther for his new field.

What the conditions were that for a time at least postponed the mission to Asia we can only guess. Perhaps hostile synagogues, warned against him by others in Galatia, closed their doors to him and threatened vigorous opposition. Certainly such hostility had already almost cost him his life at Lystra. But Paul was undoubtedly studying the missionary possibilities of Asia as he passed rapidly among its teeming cities, one of which was later to be the scene of the greatest ministry of his life.

So finding no promising opening for his message, Paul and his friends came down to Troas. There they met a young man from Philippi, who was destined to mean everything to them. He was a Greek doctor, a member of that noble profession which Hippocrates, the father of medicine, from the island of Cos, south of Miletus, had founded four centuries before. The young doctor's name was Luke. Perhaps Paul, now down on the seacoast after his journey over the uplands of Asia Minor, was stricken with malaria again and had to call a doctor. The Jews had great respect for that profession. Jeshua son of Sirach put this very plainly:

"Leave room for the physician, for the Lord has created him,

And he must not desert you, for you need him.

There is a time when your welfare depends upon them." [1]

Certainly it is a striking fact that the story of this missionary journey in The Acts now changes from the third to the first person, as if the writer himself had joined the party. Nor is there any sound reason for the doubting that he did. That is the plain meaning of the language. [2]

At Troas a great decision was reached by Paul. The gospel for which he had found no immediate opening in the province of Asia should be carried across the Ægean to Macedonia. A vision of the night decided Paul upon this course. A Macedonian stood appealing to him, and saying:

"Come over to Macedonia and help us."

Luke seems to have been from Macedonia, and as he now for a time joins the missionary party and accompanies them to Philippi, it seems clear that he had become interested in the new faith and this fact or Luke's picture of Macedonia as a missionary field prepared the way for Paul's famous vision. So out of indecision in Troas comes the resolution to transfer operations to Macedonia and begin the Christian invasion of Europe.

This was beyond doubt one of the most momentous steps Paul ever took. For he was taking Christianity out of Asia, the continent where it originated, into Europe, to which it was to make such an incalculable contribution. Did Paul realize it? Was he conscious that he was passing from one continent to another when he sailed away from

Troas with Silvanus, Timothy and Luke for the shores of Europe? Or was it just a short sea voyage to another province of the empire?

Paul was certainly empire-conscious; he was well aware that he was entering another province. But the vision of the Macedonian shows that he was conscious that a far greater step was now being taken than when he had gone from Syria to Cyprus, or from Cyprus to Galatia, or from Galatia into Asia. The ancients had long thought of Europe as a continent; the Homeric Hymn to Apollo in the seventh century before Christ speaks of it, and Herodotus in the fifth century B.C. interprets the Trojan War as a conflict between "Europe" and "Asia." [3] It is true Alexander had worked like a feverish Titan to spread Hellenism over Asia, and the Roman Empire had bound together under one authority the regions that faced each other across the Ægean, but it could not efface basic geographical divisions that had even then been recognized for centuries. Paul was well aware that he was taking the gospel into a new spiritual climate altogether. What would be the result?

The ship on which the party sailed from Troas touched, Luke tells us, at Samothrace, an Ægean island which lives in the popular mind chiefly as the place where about 305 B.C. Demetrius the "taker of cities" (Poliorcetes), as he was called, set up the beautiful and world famous statue of Victory, which was discovered there in 1863 and has ever since been the chief glory of the Louvre. Perhaps Paul saw it, but if he did, it meant to him only another evidence of the triumphant idolatry he was working to overthrow. But the mention in The Acts of the ship's touching at the island is another hint that the historian himself is now traveling with Paul and prepared to give us more details as to his journeys than we possess for his earlier movements. When Luke wrote, forty years had passed since that journey, yet his first voyage with Paul was still fresh in his mind.

On the second day they reached Macedonia, landed at Neapolis, the port of Philippi, and proceeded to Philippi, ten miles inland. The city had been a fortress of Philip of Macedon, and the base from which his son Alexander set out in 334 B.C. to invade Asia and conquer the Persian empire. More recently (42 B.C.) it had been the scene of the battle between the murderers of Cæsar and his avengers, Octavius and Anthony. Now it was a thriving Roman colony, challenging the neighboring Amphipolis for predominance in the province of Macedonia. It is very probable that it was Luke's knowledge of the city and his account of it as a promising opening for Christian missionary work that had led Paul straight to it. It was probably in Luke's house, or lodgings, that the missionaries made their first headquarters in the city.

There was no synagogue in Philippi, and after his bitter experiences with synagogue animosity in Galatia this may have influenced Paul in some measure in beginning this European mission there. Yet on the Sabbath he went to the Jewish place of prayer on the bank of the river and talked with the women who gathered there. One of them, a business woman from Thyatira in Lydia, through which the missionaries had recently passed, accepted the gospel, and became the first woman in Europe to become a Christian, as Luke was probably the first European man to do so. Her name was Lydia, and she invited the whole missionary party to make her house their home. Since Lydia was evidently a successful business woman, with a house large enough to admit three guests in addition to her own household, we may suppose it was a considerable building with the street door opening into an atrium, open in the center to the sky. Beyond this would be a peristyle court, surrounded by a second story of sleeping rooms which were reached through the gallery that ran around the court, above the columns of the peristyle.

Pansa's house in Pompeii, built in Paul's day, occupied a whole block, and contained sixty rooms on the ground floor, though half of them, facing the street and unconnected with the interior of the house, were rented for stores and shops. Lydia probably had a smaller house of similar plan. Philippi was, of course, no Pompeii, but it was far removed from the poor place it had been when Philip of Macedon gave it his name, four centuries before. The interest of the Roman emperors had fostered it, and the great east-and-west highway of the eastern empire, the Egnatian Way, passed through Philippi, which is like saying it was on a transcontinental railroad today. Perhaps its commercial advantages had drawn Lydia to it from her native Thyatira, in the heart of the province of Asia. Paul's converts who formed the church at Philippi probably gathered in the atrium or the peristyle of the house on the first day of the week, to listen to the reading of the Greek version of the Old Testament, sing their hymns, offer their prayers, and hear Paul preach. It was to be two hundred years and more before the churches could meet in buildings of their own, designed for Christian worship, and through all that time they worshiped in the private houses of their wealthier members. Of these "hosts of the church," as Paul called them, Lydia was the first in Europe.

The place of women in the Christian movement is characteristic and striking. The Jewish liturgy, in which the men of Israel thanked God they were not born women, reflected a low opinion of woman that was general in Judaism. They enjoyed a very rigidly limited access to the Temple, witnessed the synagogue service from galleries or from behind screens, but could not participate in it, and were often frowned upon in Jewish literature from Genesis, with its story of Eve, to Ecclesiastes and Ecclesiasticus, though there is a brighter picture in Proverbs.[4] But the church from the beginning welcomed women and commended them. Lydia, like Luke, had evidently felt the religious values of Judaism, and become one of the worshipers of God. She was also a business woman, with a store or shop in Philippi. Other women of affairs appear in Paul's letters and The Acts: Chloe, Phoebe, and Prisca, or Priscilla.[5]

From its beginning with the conversion of Lydia and her household, Paul's work in Philippi progressed favorably. It was interrupted through a casual contact with a very different kind of woman, a slave with the gift of ventriloquism, generally regarded in antiquity as a form of spirit possession. From what she had heard and seen of Paul and Silvanus she may have concluded that they were indeed the messengers of God they claimed to be, but it was more probably in sheer derision that she would call out at them whenever she and her masters passed them in the street.

"These men are slaves of the Most High God, and they are making known to you a way of salvation."

This brought the missionaries an unwelcome notoriety and annoyed Paul. He stood it for several days, but it happened once too often and he stopped and rebuked the woman so sternly that she subsided. Her masters, who had been making money out of her gift, found her unwilling to practice it, and turned indignantly on Paul and Silvanus for their interference. They hustled them into the public square, denouncing them as Jewish agitators, raised a mob, and succeeded in attracting the attention of the authorities, who fixed upon Paul and Silvanus as the center of the disturbance and in the summary Roman fashion had them beaten and put in jail for disturbing the peace.

This was the first time Roman authorities had interfered with Paul. But in the Philippi prison he and Silvanus did not give themselves up to bemoaning their fate, but adjusted themselves to the situation and made the best of it, praying together and singing hymns of praise. The other prisoners listened in wonder to these surprising fellow prisoners. Their behavior was still more amazing when in the middle of the night one of the earthquakes not unusual in that region shook the prison and brought the jailer rushing to the scene, to prevent what he feared might prove a general jail break, which would have meant his ruin. His dismay was such that he would have killed himself if Paul had not taken command of the situation, shouting to him that nobody had escaped, they were all there.

The result of this surprising reversal of their natural positions was that the jailer immediately realized that the missionaries were all they claimed to be. Throwing himself down before them, he asked them what he must do to be saved. They answered:

"Believe in the Lord Jesus Christ!"

Nothing in all Paul's career was more dramatic than his experience with the jailer of Philippi. The man became a Christian then and there. He washed their wounds, took them up into his house adjoining the prison, and fed and entertained them. His household accepted the new faith with him, with great rejoicing. It is clear that Paul's demeanor in the face of persecution, punishment and imprisonment made a deep impression even upon a hardened jailer. Paul himself gives us the key to his behavior when he says that he was glad to make up in his own person what was lacking in Christ's sufferings for the church, which was his body. The memory of the crucifixion and of the pathway of heroic suffering which their Master had trodden made Paul and many another primitive believer endure suffering with fortitude and actually welcome it, as part of the great necessary burden of which Christ had borne so much. They were actually his partners in the great work of redemption, sharing in his sufferings.

Next morning the magistrates sent the jailer instructions to release the missionaries, but Paul would not accept such a left-handed acquittal. He stood out for an honorable discharge. He was no fly-by-night pickup, who would slip out of jail if he found the door open, but a responsible member of society, with a great regard for his good name. He thought he had been unjustly punished and detained, and he expected complete rehabilitation. He had been subjected to a humiliating and painful punishment in public, without the opportunity of a trial, and he thought too well of the Roman Empire to regard this as a sample of its justice. He declared himself a Roman citizen and demanded that the magistrates themselves come to set him and his companion free.

The magistrates had not known that he was a citizen when they carelessly had him beaten and thrown into jail, and the news of it roused them to action. Such conduct might have serious consequences for them if it became known. They came at once in person and took Paul and Silvanus out of the prison, but requested them to leave Philippi.

Paul's insistence upon this mark of consideration was caused not by personal annoyance at his treatment, for that sort of thing he had schooled himself to expect. It was due to his sense of responsibility to his cause and his public. Christian missionaries did not belong to the kind of people that filled city prisons—cheats, cutthroats and robbers. On the contrary, they were rousing people to a loftier morality than the world had known. Besides, the people of Philippi who had followed his teaching or who might follow it must not suppose their teacher was a mere adventurer or miscreant. To secure an honorable discharge from custody was the least he could do to reassure them on that score, but that much the future of his work in Philippi required. That attained, Paul took leave of his converts and his hostess and went his way.

Paul seemed to leave Philippi a defeated man. With his work there only begun, he had been forced to leave the field. He himself was far from certain that what he had accomplished there would endure. Yet he had kindled a flame in Europe that would never go out. He had carried the gospel into a new continent which then dominated the world. He had established the first Christian church there. It was made up from the start of Greek, not Jewish, believers. Luke and Lydia were its first members, the man of medicine and letters, and the woman of affairs. Quite apart from his personal services to Paul and the Early Church, Luke was to write more than one-fourth of the New Testament, and Lydia from the very start set a splendid example of generous Christian hospitality. Philippi became the most open-handed, understanding and loyal of all Paul's churches, sending him money again and again, and in the end financing him in the long months of his final imprisonment.

CHAPTER IX 🙰 THESSALONICA TO ATHENS

IT WAS WITH heavy hearts, we may believe, that Paul, Silvanus and Timothy set out westward on the Egnatian Way, the great Roman road of the east. It led first to Amphipolis, a thriving town, the capital of that part of Macedonia, some twenty miles from Philippi. Another day's journey brought the travelers to Apollonia, thirty miles farther on, and in a day or two more they covered the thirty-eight miles to Thessalonica, at the head of the Thermaic Gulf. It was even then an ancient city, and it maintained itself through the Middle Ages and is important today. Yet in all its long history nothing has brought it quite such distinction as Paul's visit there and what came of it.

Thessalonica was the provincial capital of Macedonia, and from this time on, Paul seems to have focused his work upon great centers, from which the gospel might be expected to spread. He had not done this on his first journey, with Barnabas. He says himself in Galatians that he had first preached in Galatia because of an illness, which had driven him to the Anatolian highlands. But now, at the head of his own missionary expedition, and restored to health, he can plan his strategy. In Thessalonica his approach follows the pattern set in Galatia three years before, for he begins with the synagogue, where at first his eloquence and fervor made him as usual a welcome guest.

What followed was what we would nowadays call a

revival. Paul's preaching created immense interest among the religiously inclined people of the city. Some of the Jews accepted his doctrine that Jesus was their long-looked-for Messiah, but most of the converts were Greeks with some Jewish leanings while some women of position also came into the church. The extraordinary response the Thessalonians made to Paul's preaching was told far and wide through Macedonia and Greece, and he became famous as the man who had created such an impression in their city.

Paul never forgot the extraordinary way in which the great Christian virtues, faith, hope and love, sprang up in the hearts of the Thessalonians. Their reaction to his message filled him with gratitude. It renewed his conviction that the Spirit of God was behind his words, and gave him greater happiness than any other experience of his life. Only a few months later, in writing to the Thessalonians, he reminds them of how joyfully they had welcomed him and of how the gospel had rung out from them all over Macedonia and Greece, so that wherever he went, the news of the Thessalonian revival had gone before him. "The story of your belief in God has gone everywhere," he wrote, "so that we never need to mention it. For when people speak of us, they tell what a welcome you gave us, and how you turned from idols to God." The Thessalonians had made Paul famous in those regions, and by so much had made his way easier for him.

This encouraging success brought its own penalty, however, for it incensed the Jews and led to a riot, which centered on the house of a man named Jason who had taken the missionaries into his home. They did not find the missionaries, but dragged Jason and some other converts off to the town magistrates and charged them with disloyalty to the emperor and with disturbing the peace. Some word of Paul's earlier experiences in the synagogues of Galatia had doubtless reached the Jews of Thessalonica and caused them to identify the missionaries as men who had made trouble elsewhere.

The fear of anti-Semitic riots was ever-present in many centers of the ancient world, as we can well understand even today. The excitement and disorders occasioned by important Jewish visitors to Egypt had even led the Roman authorities to forbid such visits. No wonder Paul and Peter did not visit Egypt. It was doubtless as Jewish agitators that Paul and his companions were represented to the politarchs, as the magistrates of Thessalonica were called, and while no steps were taken against the missionaries themselves, their leading converts were put under bond to keep the peace, and Paul and his companions made haste to leave the city. Indeed, the brothers saw to it that they left at night, very much as Paul had made his first escape from Damascus some years before. So the Thessalonian mission ended as the one to Philippi had, in humiliation and retreat. What would be the fate of this little group of new converts at Thessalonica, with their Christian teachers so suddenly and disgracefully driven out of town? None of them had had more than a few weeks of Christian experience; they had no Christian literature to guide them, few if any Christian hymns to cheer them, and hardly twenty years of Christian history to inspire them. Was the faith Paul had awakened in their hearts going to survive the scorn and derision their former friends of other faiths would show toward them, after the abrupt departure of Paul and his party?

Paul's stay in Thessalonica had not been long. It is true he had found employment there, probably at his trade of tentmaking, which he resumed at Corinth a few months later, for he said afterwards that he had worked night and day at Thessalonica, in order not to burden any of the Thessalonians. He had, however, accepted money from the Philippians after he had reached Thessalonica, either before he had found work or to help support his companions Silvanus and Timothy, who may not have been so successful in self-support as Paul. From an economic point of view, Paul was a journeyman tentmaker, moving about the Roman world wherever he pleased, and having no trouble in finding work at his trade, an interesting indication of his energy and competence, as well as of the working conditions of his day.

More than fifty miles west of Thessalonica, on the great Egnatian Way, lay Berea, the most populous city of Macedonia. To it Paul and Silvanus now made their way and, undaunted by their recent experience in Thessalonica, they once more began with the synagogue. It seems as if Paul felt that sometime, somewhere, he would reach a zone of Judaism so far removed from the bigotry of Jerusalem that it would welcome the gospel message, in which he saw the fruition of the hopes of the Jewish prophets. In Berea this feeling of his was at first justified. The people of the synagogue welcomed his preaching and turned eagerly to the writings of the prophets to find out whether he was right in his use of them. Many of them accepted the gospel, as did many Greek women of position as well as Greek men too.

Once more the synagogue brought Paul in touch with these enlightened Greeks who had felt the religious values of the Jewish Scriptures but had not accepted the legal and ceremonial demands of organized Judaism.

It is clear that more than one synagogue Paul visited in his journeys had already done successful missionary work among thoughtful and sensitive Greek men and women of its community, not converting them to the Jewish faith, but yet interesting them deeply in the broader aspects of Judaism and in the Greek version of the Jewish Scriptures. It was from this outer circle of the synagogue that Paul and his fellow workers drew their most significant converts, and to this extent his missionary work rested upon that of zealous Jews who had gone before him. We read again and again of devout Greeks, the principal women, and women of position, as reached through the synagogue and interested in the Christian gospel.

The Berean mission was progressing splendidly when word of its success was carried back to Thessalonica, and the Jews from there came at once to Berea to raise the hue and cry against the missionaries. What charge they could have brought against them it is difficult to see. The cry raised at Thessalonica that Paul taught that Jesus was a king finds little support in Paul's letters, though they often speak of the Kingdom of God. In them Paul never speaks of Jesus as a king, though he does once say that Jesus must reign until he has put all enemies under his feet, and his strong belief in Jesus' speedy Second Coming to set up the Messianic era might well have seemed revolutionary. The Romans forbade the practice of new religions, but for Paul Christianity was in one sense the flowering of Judaism, and Jesus was the Messiah of the prophets, and for some time Christianity was regarded by Roman authorities simply as another sect of Judaism.

The interference of the Thessalonian Jews forced Paul to retire precipitately from the field and, escorted by some of the Berean brethren, he withdrew from Berea, leaving Silvanus and Timothy behind to arrange for the continuance of the Christian work there, while he made his way back to the coast.

It is interesting to see that these retreats of Paul's before local pressures in every case became simply the bases for new advances. If he had to leave Philippi, he advanced on Thessalonica; if he left Thessalonica, it was to find a larger field in Berea, and if he left Berea, what? The men who took Paul away from Berea went with him all the way to Athens, and left him at the very source and center of what was highest in Greek civilization.

The modern visitor to Athens is delighted with the beauty of its temples or what is left of them after the vicissitudes of more than two thousand years, for even in Paul's day the Parthenon was already nearly five hundred years old, and its magnificent location crowning the Acropolis added greatly to its impressive beauty. It dominated the city, in which one could hardly get away from it. For Paul, any thought of its architectural beauty was completely dwarfed by his sense of its idolatrous significance. It was the symbol and the actual seat of false gods and seemed to fill the city with its delusion. Paul was exasperated to behold a place so saturated with idolatry as Athens. He plunged immediately into his usual discussions in the Jewish synagogues with the Jews and the fringe of interested Greeks who always formed his best public, and talked about the gospel in the public square with such people as he could interest.

Silvanus and Timothy followed him to Athens, after putting his work in Berea on a more permanent basis, but he soon sent them back to Thessalonica and Philippi to look after matters there and to encourage the churches in those cities. He does not seem to have thought of Athens as a promising place for a Christian mission, but his street preaching brought him to the attention of some of the philosophical dilettantes who frequented Athens and its university, and they got the impression that Jesus and Resurrection were new deities he was trying to introduce. This would be a congenial idea to them, for Greek and Roman religion had conjured up a divinity to preside over every possible function or interest of human life, and altars to any others unknown who might have been missed were sometimes erected; other ancient travelers saw altars "To Unknown Gods" near Athens, and one has been found at Pergamum.[1]

New religious lecturers at Athens were supposed to appear before the council of the Areopagus, which had among its police powers the duty of passing upon their competence to speak, and Paul's philosophical hearers took him to that body for a hearing. His address before them as recorded in The Acts is a classic of tact and courage.

The scene was the King's Hall, or Portico, in the Agora, the civic center of Athens, where the council had its meetings. When Paul was called upon to give an account of what he taught, for the benefit of the members of the council, he stood up before them and said:

"Men of Athens, from every point of view I see that you are extremely religious. For as I was going about and looking at the things you worship, I even found an altar with this inscription: 'To an Unknown God.' So it is what you already worship in ignorance that I am now telling you of. God who created the world and all that is in it, since he is Lord of heaven and earth, does not live in temples built by human hands, nor is he waited on by human hands as though he were in need of anything, for he himself gives all men life and breath and everything. From one forefather he has created every nation of mankind, and made them live all over the face of the earth, fixing their appointed times and the limits of their lands, so that they might search for God, and perhaps grope for him and find him, though he is never far from any of us. For it is through union with him that we live and move and exist, as some of your poets have said,

" 'For we are also his offspring.'

"So if we are God's children we ought not to imagine that the divine nature is like gold or silver or stone, wrought by human art and thought. While God overlooked those times of ignorance, he now calls upon all men everywhere to repent, since he has fixed a day on which he will justly judge the world through a man whom he has appointed, and whom he has guaranteed to all men by raising him from the dead."

So Luke reports this dramatic address. The mention of resurrection, with which Paul's address closed, was naturally received by his audience with a good deal of derision. His argument recognized and approved the Athenians' devotion

to religion, but protested against their idolatry, appealing
to one of their own poets, Aratus, a Stoic of the third century before Christ, who wrote in his Phaenomena:

> Zeus fills the streets, the marts,
> Zeus fills the seas, the shores, the rivers!
> Everywhere our need is Zeus!
> We also are his offspring! [2]

The council evidently did not disapprove Paul's preaching in Athens, for some of them said, "We should like to
hear you again on this subject." One of them named Dionysius became a believer, as did a woman named Damaris. But
no very considerable Christian group was established as yet
in Athens, and Paul remained there for a time principally to
await the return of his messengers, Timothy and Silvanus,
from Thessalonica and Philippi. But at length he gave up
the idea of staying in Athens until they returned, and he
left the city for Corinth. He had carried the gospel through
Macedonia but had he established churches that would last?
Timothy and Silvanus would bring the answer to that question when they came.

"Slow sinks more lovely ere his race be run
Along Morea's hills the setting sun,
Not as in northern climes obscurely bright,
But one unclouded blaze of living light.
O'er the hushed deep the yellow beam he throws
Gilds the green wave that trembles as it glows.
On old Aegina's rock and Hydra's isle
The god of gladness sheds his parting smile;
O'er his own regions lingering loves to shine
Though there his altars are no more divine." [1]

SUCH THOUGHTS fill the minds of modern travelers who visit Corinth and mount to the summit of the lofty rock behind the city which formed its ancient citadel, the Acrocorinthus. But they did not fill the mind of Paul. For him the commanding fact there was the city's Greek idolatry; that was the living and hateful reality in Corinth. Paganism there was not an æsthetic memory as it was to some extent in Athens; it was a hideous present reality, one wrong more to man, one more insult to God. For in Corinth, Greek religion simply implemented and channelized sensual vices, commercializing them under the guise of worship.

The old city, destroyed by the Romans in 146 B.C., had been replaced by the new one founded by Julius Cæsar just a hundred years later as a Roman colony, and still later made the capital of Greece by Augustus. In Paul's day it was making the most of its strategic commercial position on the narrow isthmus between the Ægean and the Gulf of Corinth, with ports on both, and was on its way to becoming the metropolis of Greece, and its richest city. With all this commercial prosperity and this new architectural splendor, the worship of Aphrodite flourished in its most voluptuous and vicious forms, making Corinth a notorious seat of immorality. The mystery religions, too, were much cultivated in Corinth, and Paul later laid hold of some of their characteristic patterns to explain the values of Christian faith to the Corinthians. All in all Corinth was a stirring center of contemporary life, the meeting place of east and west, Greek and Roman, pulsing with activity, and deep in the business and the pleasures of the world.

It was to such a city so much in need of the gospel he had to preach that Paul made his way soon after his appearance before the Areopagus in Athens. He went alone, as far as we know; certainly Silvanus and Timothy were not with him, for he had sent them back to Macedonia to visit Thessalonica and Philippi and do what they could to preserve the results of his preaching in those towns. Corinth was some sixty miles from Athens, and Paul probably broke the journey at Megara, about halfway between the two cities. Or he may have gone by water, sailing from Piræus, the port of Athens, to Cenchreae, the port of Corinth on the Ægean side, a distance of less than forty miles, an easy day's sail.

In the busy city of Corinth, Paul would have no difficulty in getting a job working at his trade, and he found employment in the shop of a Jew from Pontus named Aquila, whom he doubtless met at the synagogue. Aquila and his wife, Priscilla, had recently been in Rome, but had been obliged to leave there by the orders of the Emperor Claudius.[2] So Aquila became Paul's employer. Paul went to live with Aquila and Priscilla, as he had done with Lydia in Philippi and Jason at Thessalonica, and they formed a lasting friendship. Wherever he went Paul seems to have been a welcome guest. As usual when he reached a city, he began to preach in the synagogue. Altogether matters were opening promisingly in Corinth.

But Paul's mind was not at rest. He was very anxious about his young churches in Thessalonica and Philippi. He had not been able to stay with them long enough really to establish them, he feared, and he was very apprehensive as to what effect his sudden departure so early in his work among them might have had. Had the ridicule and social persecution of their neighbors and former associates driven them to give up their new faith? It was this anxiety that had led him to send Silvanus and Timothy back from Athens to Macedonia to find out the state of the Christian groups in Philippi and Thessalonica. Even at Athens he had been hoping for news from them, and only as a last resort, when none came, did he send his companions back to the north to find out for themselves.

For the whole prospect of Paul's Greek mission hung on the result of his work in Macedonia. If it had flickered out after his abrupt departure, and it was going to be necessary to spend from six months to a year in a town to establish a church, then carrying the gospel through the empire was going to be a slow business. Desperately slow in fact, for

Paul believed the time left before the Messiah's return in judgment was very short, so short that he advised the Corinthians not to marry or separate from wife or husband, and if slaves, not to seek to be free. What did it matter? The time was so short before the end.

But if a few weeks or months of work in a Greek city could result in establishing a permanent and vigorous Christian group in it, then the gospel would go through the Greek world like wildfire. For the prospects of Paul's work everything depended on the news that Timothy and Silvanus would bring. Had the Macedonian believers held fast to their Christian profession, or had they melted away and drifted back into Judaism or paganism? Paul took up his work in the synagogue at Corinth with a mind full of distress and fear that all his labor in Macedonia had been lost, and his missionary experiment in a new continent had failed.

The arrival of Silvanus and Timothy finally put an end to these apprehensions, for they brought him wonderful news. His churches in Macedonia had stood firm. His abrupt departure had not shaken them at all. The Thessalonians in particular had never doubted him or his message. They had gone through some hard times, it is true. They had had to bear the same kind of ill treatment from their neighbors that the first Jewish Christians had sustained from the Jews, back in Palestine. They had missed Paul just as much as he had missed them, and wanted nothing so much as to have him come back and visit them again.

It was in the spring of A.D. 50 that Paul had come to Corinth and to that date we can accordingly assign the letter that he wrote to the Thessalonians to express his intense relief and his reaction to Timothy's good news. What Silvanus reported we do not know, but from other sources it is clear that the church at Philippi was standing firm. In fact, in writing to the Philippians some years later, Paul remarks that about this time they had sent him a gift of money. "And you at Philippi," he wrote, "know as well as I do, that in the early days of the good news, after I left Macedonia, no church but yours went into partnership and opened an account with me. Even when I was at Thessalonica you sent money more than once for my needs." So while Timothy brought splendid news from the young church at Thessalonica, Silvanus probably brought something more substantial from the church at Philippi.

Yet the Thessalonians, too, made a contribution of the most substantial kind to our Christian heritage, for the letter that Paul immediately wrote and sent them they faithfully preserved, probably in their church chest, in which the early churches soon began to keep the scrolls from which they read in church, and any cups, plates and vestments they came to use only for their religious rites. So these earliest of Paul's letters, our I and II Thessalonians, were preserved at Thessalonica and eventually passed into the first collection of Paul's letters, made and published a generation later.

First Thessalonians gives us our first direct contemporary glimpse of the mind of Paul, and of the life and thought of the Early Church, only twenty years after the death of Jesus. The value of personal letters for historical study is admittedly very great, for they give us not what some later historian thought happened, or what some contemporary apologist wished people to suppose happened, but what actually passed between the missionary and his converts; what memories he cherished, what fears he admitted, what problems he sought to solve, what doctrines he taught, what attitudes he assumed toward them. In I Thessalonians we see primitive Christianity in actual operation, and we get a clear and striking picture of Paul himself in his relations with his converts. In fact, we may regard the letter as a striking bit of autobiography. It is, of course, overshadowed in the collection of Paul's letters by the greater letters to Galatia, Corinth and Rome, but if we had none of these we would yet possess in I Thessalonians an invaluable picture of Paul the missionary in his relations with the people of his ministry. For the life of Paul, what could be more valuable than an account from his own hand of the thoughts and feelings that possessed his mind in the early days of his great Corinthian mission?

Paul associates his missionary companions with himself in writing to the Thessalonians. Timothy and Silvanus had worked with him in Thessalonica, and they join him in writing the letter. He breaks out immediately with the gratitude he always feels for the amazing response they had given his preaching when he first preached in Thessalonica. Their response had been so ready and sincere. They had taken up the new faith with such enthusiasm that the news of their acceptance of it had spread all over Macedonia and Greece and prepared Paul's way before him in other cities. When people spoke of Paul it was to say, "Oh yes, he is the man who had such a wonderful reception when he preached at Thessalonica!"

Some slanders had indeed arisen about Paul after his departure. Stories had been circulated against him, to undermine him with his converts—that he was a man of corrupt life, or wanted to make money out of his converts, or simply to get a following to satisfy his vanity. Paul repels these charges, probably brought to him by Timothy, and refers to his policy of self-support, his fatherly attitude to them, his irreproachable relations with them all. How intensely he had wanted to go back and revisit them, but that had not been possible! He is deeply attached to them. "For what hope or happiness shall we have or what prize to be proud of in the presence of our Lord Jesus when he comes, except you? You are our pride and our joy."

He tells of his anxiety, culminating in his sending his messenger Timothy back to encourage them to meet such persecutions as might overtake them with firmness and courage. Now that Timothy has returned and brought him such wonderful news of their faith and love, and of their unwavering devotion to Paul himself, he feels greatly encouraged: "Now I can really live, since you are standing firm in the Lord." How can he thank God enough for them!

He reminds them of their Christian obligations, of purity of life, practical brotherly love, and industrious self-support. He sets forth his belief in the return of Christ from heaven and the necessity of being ready at any time for it. They must respect their leaders, live at peace with one another, treat everyone with kindness, and listen to the voice of the Spirit in their hearts. The whole letter breathes an air of warm affection and deep religious concern for them. This was the atmosphere of Paul's churches, at their best. He and they were united in a glowing spiritual fellowship of mutual affection and good will. It is a happy circumstance that the earliest of his letters that has come down to us reflects this, for situations arose later in Corinth and Galatia that stirred Paul to great vehemence and sharp rebuke. Indeed, even at Thessalonica a few weeks later a situation arose that led him to express himself sternly.

Paul's preaching of Jesus as the promised Messiah of Jewish expectation seemed to carry with it the idea that the Day of the Lord, so repeatedly spoken of by the prophets from Amos on, had come, and with it the end of the old era and the beginning of the Messianic age. Or perhaps Paul's preaching of the speedy return of Christ was so convincing that men felt that the only thing worth doing was to prepare for it. At any rate, some of the believers at Thessalonica were so moved that they had given up working for a living and were devoting themselves to getting ready for the end. But as time wore on, they became a charge upon the charity of their brethren in the church and finally, since they could not devote all their idleness to profitable religious exercises, a nuisance and a scandal. They became idlers and busybodies.

At first Paul had counseled the Thessalonians to provide for any brother who was in need, and acknowledged that they were already doing it most generously, not only in Thessalonica but all over Macedonia.[3] It is interesting to find this practical note struck in this earliest piece of Christian literature. Even then, however, Paul urged the Thessalonians to support themselves and mind their own affairs, so as to have the respect of the outsiders and not be dependent upon anyone. But the situation did not improve but grew worse and worse. When Paul learned of this, he wrote a second letter to them, qualifying his doctrine of the speedy and unexpected coming of Christ with the Jewish doctrine of the Antichrist, who would come first and win a great following for his false doctrines by his pretended wonders, only to be soon defeated and destroyed by the coming of the true Messiah.[4] Paul felt that the preliminary tokens of the Antichrist's coming were already discernible in what was going on in the world about him, but that something, perhaps the authority of the empire, was temporarily holding him in check. But soon that restraining force would give way, the Antichrist, the embodiment of evil, would begin his brief ascendancy and then meet the true Christ in the great final encounter between the champions of right and wrong. So Jewish thought had dramatized the age-long conflict of good and evil.

Paul still commends the Thessalonians, for he knows that only a small part of their number has fallen into idleness and its vices. He warns them to avoid such idlers and remember his example of hard work and self-support. He reminds them that he had told them, "If anyone refuses to work, give him nothing to eat!" Yet they are not to be too hard upon the idler: "Do not look upon him as an enemy but warn him as a brother." He prays that peace may be restored and prevail among them.

These letters were intended solely for the Thessalonian believers in the situations of the moment. They were written and sent with no thought of their ever being thought of as Scripture, or even published. So at Corinth, in A.D. 50, Paul quite unconsciously began Christian literature. But we must not suppose that much of Paul's attention at Corinth was given to the writing of letters. There as always his great concern was preaching the gospel. Even before his messengers had come over from Macedonia, he was deep in his engrossing work among the Corinthians. He had begun as usual in the synagogue, but as usually happened, few of the Jews there accepted his gospel and he had soon to find another place to preach. It is true that Crispus, the leader of the synagogue, and his household accepted the gospel, and Paul says in I Corinthians that he himself baptized Crispus,[5] as he did a Greek or Roman convert to Judaism named Titius Justus. This man lived next door to the synagogue and Paul soon transferred his public meetings to a room in his house.[6] Jewish opposition had driven him from the synagogue, but not from the city and not even from the neighborhood. It was an anxious time. Everywhere else expulsion from the synagogue had been followed by a relentless persecution that had finally driven him from the place. But in Corinth, reinforced by a vision, Paul stood his ground. At last, in one city he was able to stay long enough to establish a church as he thought it should be established. He settled in Corinth, and for a year and a half continued his work.

In the summer or autumn of A.D. 51 a new governor came out as usual from Rome to Greece and took up his residence in Corinth. His name was Gallio, and he was the elder brother of the Stoic philosopher Seneca. It must have been soon after his arrival that the Jews, who had never become reconciled to Paul's presence and work in Corinth, had him brought before Gallio, since there was always a possibility that the new governor's inexperience or weakness might yield them the satisfaction that his predecessor had refused. Gallio, however, was a much stronger man than they supposed. He made short work of their appeal and drove them from the court. Pliny, Tacitus and Dio Cassius all speak of Gallio, who fell sick in Corinth, and took a sea voyage after his year of office there, complaining that it was the climate that had made him ill. As a final gesture the Jews seized Sosthenes, the leader of the synagogue, and beat him before the tribunal, but Gallio paid no attention to it. Gallio was put to death by Nero's orders twelve or fifteen years later (64 or 66); indeed Nero wiped out all three brothers, Gallio, Seneca and Mela, the last the father of the poet Lucan.

It is this clash with Gallio that enables us to date I Thessalonians and Paul's coming to Corinth so definitely. For the Gallio incident evidently took place toward the end of Paul's stay in Corinth and also soon after Gallio came there to begin his year of office as proconsul of Greece, and that, a Delphi inscription has shown, was in the summer or autumn of A.D. 51.[7] But not long after the incident Paul left Corinth after a stay of eighteen months, so that his arrival there must have been early in 50. As he wrote I Thessalonians very soon after his arrival in Corinth, in fact as soon as Timothy overtook him there, it must have been written in the spring of that year.

Paul's Jewish opponents in Corinth must have turned upon Sosthenes in vexation that he had failed in presenting their case against Paul to Gallio. Sosthenes ended by going over to Paul's side and becoming a Christian, like the other synagogue leader of whom we know, Crispus, who was one of the two Corinthians Paul himself had baptized. Later on, in Ephesus, Paul associates Sosthenes with himself in writing I Corinthians.

These events did not hurry Paul's departure from Corinth, where for the first time he had the opportunity to establish a vigorous church. How vigorous it was, his later correspondence with it—his longest known correspondence with one church—clearly shows. The church at Corinth must have been full of strenuous religious personalities, decided people, eager for all the gospel had to give of gifts and endowments, rights and hopes. We may be glad of this, for it called forth all Paul's resources of explanation and intuition, and in the end immensely enriched the literature of religion. The Corinthians sometimes tried his patience almost to the breaking point, it is true, but even that led to richer and fuller disclosures of religious truth on his part, and revealed Paul himself and his motives and methods as no others of his letters did. The same traits that are later reflected in his letters we may suppose were already showing themselves to some extent during Paul's stay in Corinth, where he at last encountered the Greek mind in religion, in all its tireless effervescent vivacity and vigor.

CHAPTER XI 🙥 REPORT TO ANTIOCH

ALMOST THREE years had now passed since Paul had been in Antioch and had an opportunity of conferring with the Christian leaders there. He had achieved a momentous advance in the Christian missionary movement, on which he might well wish to report to his original sponsors in that city. He had carried the gospel into Europe and into the very heart of Greece itself, and he had met with a most gratifying success. He must also learn more definitely and in more detail than letters could inform him of the general progress of Christian work about the eastern Mediterranean; was it moving into the north, the south and the east with the same success it was meeting in the west? This world-wide mission must be held together by frequent meetings among its leaders, and its headquarters were still in Syria and Palestine.

Paul left Corinth by the port of Cenchreae, on its Ægean side, for he was sailing for Ephesus. At Cenchreae a Nazirite vow he had made reached its fulfillment and he cut his hair in recognition of the fact.[1] Jewish ways still clung to him, as his later differences with the Corinthians all too clearly showed.[2] With Aquila and Priscilla, who were transferring their business to Ephesus, he sailed from Cenchreae one day in the early autumn of A.D. 51 for Ephesus, two hundred and fifty miles due east of Corinth.

Paul had already looked longingly upon the province of

Asia as a possible mission field, but had been led to turn away from Ephesus and cross to Macedonia instead. Now he found it possible to reconnoiter the ancient Ionian city as a field for missionary effort. His stay in Ephesus was short, but he went to the synagogue and was well received. The Jews were interested in his message, and even wished him to stay on, but he felt he must hasten back to Antioch. After assuring them of his intention to return, he sailed from Ephesus for the east.

In Antioch, Paul must have had a wonderful reunion with his old missionary colleagues as he reported on his extraordinary success in carrying the gospel into Europe and establishing it in the chief centers of Macedonia and Greece.[3] Some of this information had no doubt reached the church at Antioch before, through letters from Paul and his colleagues. But now he is able to present it in person in his graphic manner, and great must have been the joy of the missionary-minded Christians of Antioch as they learned of the continuing success of their great experiment in sending the gospel to the Greek communities of the west. The response of the Greeks in Antioch to their preaching there years before had been a true index of Greek interest in the gospel everywhere about the empire, and Paul's visit must have been in this respect a very happy and hopeful one.

If Paul had news for Antioch, Antioch had news for him too, and not all of it good news. The Jews of Jerusalem were growing more and more turbulent and disorderly, and for Paul, who regarded the Roman authority as a social safeguard, this was distressing. News from Palestine nowadays is not unlike what Paul must have heard in Antioch in the year 51–52.

Much more disquieting was the news from his nearer missions in the uplands of Asia Minor, where he had planted the gospel in the face of such bitter opposition four or five years before. For the ultra-Jewish group which Paul had encountered and driven from the field in Antioch had shifted its attack to the mission field and was meeting with marked success in the churches of Galatia, in Derbe, Lystra, Iconium and Pisidian Antioch. This movement, which had its origin in Jerusalem—perhaps with the sanction of James himself, for his emissaries were held responsible for it—had shown itself in Antioch, where it had swayed even Peter and Barnabas for a time, as we have seen. But Paul's straight thinking and hard hitting had seemed to put a stop to this effort to entangle the Christian believers with the legal heritage of Judaism and make the synagogue the gateway to the church.

In Galatia the Judaizers had taken advantage of Paul's absence in Macedonia and Greece to undermine his position and his teaching. He was not, they explained, one of the twelve apostles, indeed he was no "apostle" at all. He had no authority to reduce the requirements for admission to the church, in order to make them more agreeable to heathen applicants. Jesus had completed and carried out the old covenant or agreement between God and Abraham, and the spiritual blessings he had brought were for the heirs of that agreement. Outsiders could be incorporated into that body of heirs by well-known methods that had long been in vogue. They should be circumcised and undertake the observance of the Jewish Law, or at least the essential features of it. The Christian salvation, these teachers felt, was a monopoly of the Jewish people and could be had only on their terms, and these were the terms. Nothing had happened to alter them or justify anyone in altering them. The Judaistic teachers now called upon the Galatian converts to conform to these requirements or give up their claims to the Christian salvation.

This news which reached Paul at Antioch, very probably as soon as he arrived there, stirred him as he had never been stirred before. The attack upon himself and the genuineness of his commission as an apostle struck at one of the deepest of his convictions, the reality of his call to preach the gospel to the heathen. It also threatened to undo what he knew to be a real and vital experience on the part of the Galatian Christians and to distort the Christian experience into the old lifeless regimentation which had tortured his early years. The new faith which Christ had opened to mankind would, if these teachers had their way, wither into nothing but another sect of the old subjection to the letter of the Law and the old jejune regimentation of conduct, harsh, narrow and exclusive, with no soil at all for what he saw were the true fruits of the spirit of Christ—love, joy, peace, patience, kindness, goodness, faithfulness, gentleness, self-control. The Judaizers' teaching was simply the denial of all these things, and their invasion of Galatia with their doctrine threatened to smother the Christian faith in its very infancy.

Paul must have wanted above everything else to go at once to Galatia and set this matter right in no uncertain way. But if he had just arrived in Antioch he could hardly do this.

There were matters on which he must have wished to confer with his old sponsors in Antioch. Most of all, he must tell them of all that had happened in Macedonia and Greece and of the great new future opening before the Christian Church in the thriving and historic cities about the Ægean. His own religious experience had deepened and widened in the course of this work. His faith was deeper and stronger, his love greater and his hope higher. His preaching had found a response such as it had never met before. He had much to say to his old friends in Antioch, and he must stay with them at least a little while.

So once more he resorts to a letter. He had already done this at least twice in Corinth, when the situation in Thessalonica had stirred him to write. Now, as then, he dictated it to an amanuensis, and after it was written out, read it and added a postscript in his own hand. It gives us an amazing glimpse of what Paul was thinking there at Antioch. It is a blaze of fiery indignation from beginning to end. Stiff traditional versions give little idea of the torrent of feeling, argument and reminiscence that constitutes the letter to the Galatians.

The very words of the salutation with which Greeks began their letters threw down the gauntlet to the Judaizers in Galatia. He *is* an apostle, and no mere emissary of the Twelve; his commission comes directly from Christ and God, through inner conviction and experience. Nor is he alone. All the brothers who are with him are behind what he has to say to the Christians of Galatia. He is speaking not only for himself but for the great missionary church at Antioch, from which the gospel had come to them.

Paul's mind is full of amazement and indignation. It is not the gospel at all that their new teachers are preaching; they have turned it completely around and merit the curse of God for so doing. Paul's gospel had come to him, he fully believed, by a revelation of Christ himself. He did not owe it to any human informant from Jerusalem. His contact with Jerusalem since his conversion had been limited to two short visits. On the first of these he saw of the Jerusalem leaders only Cephas and James; on the second, fourteen years later, this very matter of the heathen converts' relation to the Law had been taken up and settled by the recognition of their freedom from all legal requirements, including circumcision. The only stipulation was that the Greek churches should contribute money for the support of the poor Christians in Jerusalem, to which Paul readily agreed. The Jerusalem leaders had then pledged him their full coöperation, although later at Antioch, James's emissaries had led the Jewish Christians there to give up eating with Gentile believers, until Paul stepped in and showed them their inconsistency. On both occasions he had won the day over those who sought to entangle his Greek converts in the endless and lifeless snarl of Jewish ceremonial law.

The Jewish Christians themselves had found their religious satisfaction not in their old legalistic observances but in faith in Christ. They had needed that faith just as much as the heathen had. The Galatians must have lost their senses. Had obeying the minute details of the ceremonial law brought them the consciousness of the Spirit's presence and guidance? On the contrary, that consciousness had never come to them until they had begun to exercise faith.

Even Abraham owed his acceptance with God to his faith, and his true spiritual heirs are the men of faith. The most the Law had done was to lay men under its curse for failing to observe it fully. From that curse Christ's death had ransomed them and opened the way for the heathen to receive the blessing long ago given to Abraham.

Arguments of every kind jostle each other in the mind of Paul. How can the Law, given centuries later, be brought into the covenant with Abraham, made four hundred years before Moses' time? The men of faith are the heirs of that older covenant, which cannot be invalidated by the Law. As for the Law, it was later, subordinate and temporary, and seemed to Paul to have done little but make men at least conscious of their own guilt and so ready for redemption. Yes, the Law had served a certain purpose like that of the ancient attendant who looked after a boy on his way to school and saw him safely into his teacher's hands. So the Law has guided them into the presence of their true teacher Christ. Once there, they have no need of the Law any more. In Christ Jesus they are all sons of God through their faith. The old distinctions of Jew and Greek, slave and free, male and female, no longer mean anything, in religion. In union with Christ they are all one. In his prayer book the Jew still thanks God that he was not born a Gentile, a slave or a woman. Paul had done with such shallow egotism, and with splendid breadth declared the Christian church open to all mankind, regardless of nationality, sex or class.

Like the noble child, taken to his teacher, the Christian is the heir of a great inheritance. Until the boy comes of age, he and his affairs are in the hands of others, but when he does, he is free and his own master, and so the Christian is a son and heir and can call God Father. In an impassioned appeal Paul asks the Galatians how they can possibly turn back from such a religious destiny to such material matters as observing the Jewish calendar of holy days, feasts and seasons, which for Greeks not brought up in them could be only artificial religious expressions, with no basis in inner experience.

From this rapid fire of varied arguments Paul's mind turned to the personal side. How warmly the Galatians had welcomed him when he first appeared among them, sick and miserable as he was. Then they welcomed him as a messenger from God, even as Christ himself. What has happened to turn them against him now? The men who have been undermining him in Galatia have their own ends to serve. They mean to make the Galatians dependent upon them for salvation and admission to the church. That is why they claim as their prerogative the right to fix the terms on which the Christian salvation is to be had. Religious control of the Galatians is what they are aiming at. If only Paul could see them in person and talk to them!

The very Scripture they read, allegorically understood, will show them where they stand. For Isaac was not Abraham's only son; he had another, by the slave girl Hagar. They may symbolize two lines of descent, one, to slavery to the Law; the other, to freedom in the Spirit. This last is what Christ has called us to, for as men of faith we are the true heirs of Abraham's faith and Isaac's freedom. This is the freedom with which Christ has freed us.

With this trumpet call to freedom Paul's argument culminates. No law can bind the Christian; he is free! It is no use trying to combine this freedom with fifty per cent law or some other proportion of it. The Christian is absolutely free, or he is not free at all. The moment the Galatians accept even a modicum of Jewish Law they have sacrificed their freedom, finished with Christ and lost God's favor. The man who has been unsettling their faith will have to pay the penalty for it, whoever he is.

But freedom is always dangerous, for it may degenerate into license. Yet there is no real difficulty in telling when the Spirit is genuinely at work, for its fruits are love, joy, peace, patience, kindness, goodness, faithfulness, gentleness, self-control! These cannot be mistaken. The believer is to yield himself to the Spirit's guidance, in unwearying devotion.

When Paul read the letter over, as copied out by the professional letter writer to whom he had dictated it, he could not refrain from adding in his own larger handwriting a few matters already touched on in the letter, which he wanted to underline. He appeals to the scars of his beating at Philippi as marking him unmistakably as a slave of Christ.

These were the thoughts that filled Paul's mind at Antioch, where years before he had fought out this battle of the Greek-Christian's religious freedom.

Galatians is Christianity's first great contribution to religious literature. It was far more than a friendly, helpful, pastoral letter to a group of Christian congregations. It was a revolutionary statement of religious ideals and attitudes. Paul believed the Christian Church was open on equal terms to Greeks and Jews, yes, men and women, and even slaves and freemen. In such women as Lydia, Damaris, and Priscilla in Macedonia and Greece, Paul had found devoted followers of Christ. They are not to be excluded from the Christian congregations as Jewish women were from sharing in the worship of the synagogue. Greek mystery religions had long admitted slaves and women to initiation, and this Greek breadth in religion is matched in Paul's conception of the all-embracing church. In some letters Paul has a special message for the slave members.[4] In after years they were to be bishops and prophets in the churches.[5]

It is as a great charter of freedom in religion that Galatians is most notable. The Christian's guide is not a book but a spirit. He is bound not by rules but by his inner consciousness of the mind of Christ. The experience of faith is his introduction to this guidance, which transcends any regulations of law or Scripture and insures a life acceptable to God.

With no thought of being autobiographical in his argument with the Galatians, Paul throws important light upon his labors and movements in the early years of his Christian mission. And what a preacher he must have been, for Galations, with its occasional bursts of feeling and its scarcely organized wealth of argument of every kind gives us some idea of the power, variety and vigor with which Paul must have spoken in his sermons and discussions in Philippi, Thessalonica and Corinth. With a trenchant logic he deals with his own contacts with Jerusalem, his and their religious experience, the story of Abraham, the words of Scripture, the true place of the Law in Jewish experience, the dignity of Christian sonship, the selfish aims of the Judaizers, the freedom of the Christian in religion, the fruits of the Spirit.

These were the thoughts that filled Paul's mind in the first days after he reached Antioch, and this was the letter Paul sent by some trusty messenger over the Taurus Mountains from Antioch to the churches of Derbe, Lystra, Iconium and Pisidian Antioch, to undo the grievous harm the Judaizers were doing among them. The fact that they cherished and preserved his letter is sufficient proof of its effect and success. Paul had found a powerful instrument for dealing with distant situations which he was to use again and again with telling effect.

PAUL'S VISIT to Antioch was no doubt shortened by the situation in Galatia, and as soon as he reasonably could, and without waiting for an answer to his letter, he followed it to the scene. Once more he made the now familiar journey by way of Tarsus through the Cilician Gates to the upland of Anatolia and the well-remembered Galatian cities, Lystra, Derbe, Iconium, and Pisidian Antioch, the scenes of his earlier humiliations and successes. The task of restoring the Galatians to reliance upon faith for their salvation had to be completed, but his powerful letter had undoubtedly done much to convince them. His firm conviction and vigorous eloquence hastened their deliverance from the mischievous persuasions of the Judaizers and set their feet once more upon the way of faith. This was his third visit to that region, and the last time the people were to see the great apostle in Galatia. But Paul probably did not prolong his visit to his old friends there, for he was anxious to go on from them to the shores of the Ægean and begin the work at Ephesus which he had planned when he had touched there on his way to Antioch.

Meantime, a new and brilliant figure had appeared upon the Christian scene in Ephesus. A Jew named Apollos had come up from Alexandria, presented himself at the synagogue and made an immediate impression. He was a fine example of Alexandrian Judaism, learned, eloquent, and zealous. The Jews of Alexandria had long since translated the Hebrew Scriptures into Greek and produced most of the books known to us as the Apocrypha. The greatest figure among them, the philosopher Philo, had probably just passed away, after an extraordinary career of authorship. His voluminous works, written in Greek, included an elaborate allegorization of Jewish laws, and the doctrine of a divine Logos (Word, Reason) as the medium of God's revelation to men. Apollos must have known him; certainly he knew his works, though allegory was a favorite interpretative instrument among Greeks as well as Jews, as Epictetus a generation later was to show.

The high spiritual level of Alexandrian Jewish thought is admirably shown in the so-called Wisdom of Solomon, a fine religious poem written some ten years before Apollos' arrival in Ephesus. Altogether, the Jewish environment from which Apollos came was the finest Jewish atmosphere of the day, much loftier than that of the Judaism of Palestine, which was degenerating into violence and disorder. He had also heard, probably in Alexandria, of John the Baptist's preaching of repentance and of a mightier One to come, and it was this teaching that he presented with great fervor in the synagogue at Ephesus. There Aquila and Priscilla, Paul's old friends from Corinth, heard him and, seeing the imperfect character of his message, they took him home with them and told him the sequel of John's work, in the ministry and teaching of Jesus, with all that had followed. Apollos accepted the gospel. A little later, when he crossed the Ægean to Corinth he carried a letter of introduction to the church there and soon became the foremost Christian preacher in Corinth. Evidently a little group of believers had already gathered about Aquila and Priscilla, to form the nucleus of the church of Ephesus.

Meantime, Paul had concluded his work of correcting the Judaistic tendency among the Galatians and moved on to Ephesus to begin his gospel mission there. Among the first people he met was a group of Johannists, who like Apollos had heard of John's preaching and accepted it, and when Paul told them of the work of Jesus, they joyfully accepted him as indeed the greater One who was to come. About Aquila and Priscilla and this group of former Johannists now rapidly gathered under Paul's preaching the men and women who were soon to make the church of Ephesus for a time the greatest of Christian churches.

Paul began as usual in the synagogue and met with such success that it was three months before he felt obliged to find another place to preach in. As he had done in Corinth, now again in Ephesus he got the use of a lecture hall, that of Tyrannus, and there for two years he continued to preach daily, until his historian could say that everyone in Asia, Greeks as well as Jews, had heard the gospel message. Ephesus was a great center of life in Asia. It was the largest and most flourishing city and the principal port of Asia, which was considered the richest province of the empire. It had suffered from an earthquake in A.D. 21, but had been spendidly restored, with the aid of the Emperor Tiberius. Among the great cities of the empire, it ranked after Rome, Alexandria and Antioch. Its magnificent open-air theater seated 24,500 spectators, and its great temple of the Asian goddess Artemis was one of the Seven Wonders of the World. It was not on the Maeander River, to the winding course of which we owe our word "meander," but much of the river's commerce reached the sea through Ephesus, to save following the river's windings down to its mouth at Miletus. The world-wide interest in the worship of Artemis and gifts to her famous shrine had made her temple a considerable banking and safe-deposit center. If not actually the capital of Asia, Ephesus was the center of the emperor worship of the province and the new proconsul always made his entry into his province there.

Once more Paul made his home no doubt with Aquila and Priscilla, and the first congregation that formed in Ephesus met in their house. Paul's program in Ephesus was an intensely busy one. Like other workmen in the Greek world, he got up very early in the morning, by daylight or before, and put in the long hours of the Greek working day in the shop of Aquila and Priscilla, which was probably in their house or attached to it. The late afternoon, which the Greeks devoted to relaxation, athletics, theaters, and the like, and probably the evening also, he spent preaching in the lecture hall of Tyrannus and holding discussions with inquirers. These addresses and debates attracted a great deal of attention in Ephesus; visitors to the city from other parts of Asia were drawn to them and carried back his message to the neighboring towns. It was in this way that the gospel began to spread from Ephesus over the whole province. Asia was a thickly populated region, full of thriving cities, rich in historic memories, Miletus, Smyrna, Sardis, Troas, Pergamum, but the lively Greeks who filled their streets cared less for the past than for the present and the future, and it was of these that Paul had most to say.

Ephesus was a thriving port, and ships were constantly going and coming to and from the other port cities about the Ægean, especially Corinth, only two or three days' sail across the sea. So Paul was soon again in communication with his old friends at Corinth and got news of them and from them. In this way he learned that some members of the Corinthian church were still practicing their old pagan vices—greed, idolatry, avarice, drunkenness and immorality —and were yet retaining their places in the Christian body unrebuked. This stirred him to send a short letter to the Corinthians calling upon them to have nothing to do with such people, for such practices could have no place in the church.[1]

Before Paul had word of the effect of this letter upon the Corinthians, he had news of the church there from other Corinthian visitors to Ephesus. Some people connected with a woman named Chloe, perhaps her slaves or agents, came to see him and told him all the news of the Corinthian church. And very bad news it was, in Paul's opinion. The Corinthians were breaking up into cliques and factions, not because they differed seriously among themselves about any doctrine or practice, but simply because some preferred Apollos' style of preaching to Paul's, while others liked Paul's forceful but less elegant diction better than that of Apollos. The Greeks were always too much inclined to factions, and this trait clung to them even after they joined the Christian Church. Apollos, coming from Alexandria, the intellectual center of first-century Judaism, was a more finished literary preacher than Paul, whose diction was much more direct and rugged. Some Corinthians went so far as to say that Paul was quite lacking in eloquence. Others had heard of Cephas, that is, Peter, and his important place in Jerusalem and Antioch, and liked to consider themselves his followers. Still others refused any minor allegiance and declared themselves followers of Christ. So at least four parties were dividing the Corinthian church.

Another distressing thing these people told Paul was that the Corinthian Christians were taking their business differences with one another to the heathen law courts for settlement. Paul had no respect for such law courts. He believed the whole heathen system, social and civil, was doomed to early and well-merited destruction; only the general fabric of the empire he believed was being permitted to stand temporarily as a check on the Antichrist. He was horrified that members of the Kingdom of God would so far recognize the system as to submit anything to its civil courts, to which he considered the Christian brotherhood far superior.

Paul was further distressed by the account Chloe's people gave him of the way the Lord's Supper was being observed in Corinth, where its solemn religious character was being lost in feasting and drunkenness. The Corinthians, accustomed to the common meals of the mystery religions, made it the occasion for entertaining one another, bringing an abundance of food and drink, and breaking into small dinner parties, from which the poorer brothers were left out. So at some tables there was not enough to eat and drink; at others there was eating and drinking to excess.

Besides all this, immoral behavior was beginning to appear among the Corinthians; one man had married his widowed stepmother, which seemed to Paul an indecent and wicked act. All in all, the Corinthian church was falling into unendurable laxity and confusion, although it was hardly a year since Paul had left.

Paul's mind was already seething with all these disorders reported to him from Corinth when there came one day into his shop or lodging at Ephesus three men from the Corinthian church, sent by it expressly to consult him. They were Stephanas, Achaicus and Fortunatus. Stephanas was apparently the leader of the Corinthian church and the man who presided over its meetings and conducted them. They brought Paul a letter from the Corinthian church, the only one that we know that he received, though he must have had many. It may be thought of as an answer to the one he had written the Corinthians, though it really raised a number of new questions. It was a veritable question box, full of the kind of problems that confronted the church in the Greek world.

Paul's converts generally found it natural and helpful to bring their practical religious problems to him for solution. They looked up to him not only as the one who had brought the gospel to them and introduced them to the Christian faith, but as a man of sound judgment and great understanding of the mind of Christ, whom they could consult with confidence. That was why the Corinthians laid this extraordinary list of questions before him for his counsel and direction. They did not think of him as a religious authority whose word would be law to them; they were too independent for that. But they had seen enough of him in his long stay in Corinth to be convinced of the value of his thinking on these or any other questions where religion was concerned.

We do not possess the Corinthians' letter to Paul, but from his reply to it, in our I Corinthians, it can be outlined. The Corinthians wanted to know what to do about marriage and divorce. Paul had taught them to expect the end of their age to come very soon, perhaps in a few months or years. How did this affect the matter of getting married? And if people were unhappily married, or married to unbelievers, what then? Should they separate? Should engaged couples marry?

The Corinthians had always found the best meat in Corinth in the markets attached to the idol temples. The great shrines of Corinth were those of Aphrodite, the goddess of love, and of Poseidon, the god of the sea, whose temple is still standing in Corinth. Now that these Corinthians had become Christians, they no longer visited these temples as worshipers. But some of them continued to get their meat at the temple markets, for they were the best markets in the city and supplied better meat than could be bought elsewhere. These people argued that they had knowledge, and it told them that the idols were nothing and it did not matter at all that the animals had been killed in sacrifice to them. The prayer of thanksgiving that they uttered over their food consecrated it and they felt that they had a perfect right to go on buying the best meat in Corinth, as they had always done. Other Corinthians, however, felt that the problem was a deeper one. The money paid for the meat at the temple markets helped to maintain the abominable practices of heathenism, and made the patrons of these markets contributors to the support of idolatry. Moreover, if they kept up their old practice of buying their meat at the temples, would they not soon be giving their dinners in the temple clubrooms, as they had formerly done? That would be a scandal in the church and might lead them back to full participation in their old idolatrous practices. Such problems must have arisen in many early Christian groups, which had problems of social adjustment to make, quite as real and difficult as those faced by Jewish believers in their relation to the various aspects of the Jewish Law.

A whole series of questions was raised by the matter of Christian worship. They met, as we have seen, in such private houses as were large enough to accommodate a meeting and were available for such use. Women came as well as men, a decided contrast to Jewish synagogue practice. How should the women dress? Were they guests in a private house or spectators in a public place? Admission of women to some of the mystery religions had brought women somewhat increased freedom, and the Christian Church already contained many able and intelligent women. How should the women of Corinth dress for church?

Another question that was disturbing the Corinthians was how far to permit their meetings to be disturbed by speaking with tongues or, as we should call it, ecstatic speaking. Then as now people of unstable emotional types, when carried away by religious excitement, would break out into an uncontrollable babbling; as such moods are infectious, others would join in, and the meeting be thrown into confusion.

Yet this ecstatic speaking seemed to the Corinthians a

genuine religious expression, and they hesitated to forbid it altogether. How could it be regulated or controlled?

The letter from Corinth which Paul now set out to answer [2] was in part no doubt an answer to his earlier one, already mentioned. But in answering it Paul first took occasion to speak his mind in no uncertain terms about the bad news recently brought him by the people of Chloe. Of the justice of their charges he could satisfy himself by consulting Stephanas and his party. He condemns the factions at Corinth, declines to be put in a position of rivalry with Apollos or Cephas, and defends his simplicity of language as best fitted to the capacities of the Corinthians. He denounces the immoral practices of which he had been told and calls upon the Corinthians to give up their habit of going to law with one another. Indeed, he had written them a letter on these shortcomings of theirs longer than I Thessalonians before he turned to the subject of their letter at all.

It is in the way in which Paul takes up their questions that he reveals himself most fully and attractively as a religious thinker and teacher. Nothing was farther from his mind than to substitute a new legislation for the old one or to pose as a Christian lawgiver. His Christianity was no matter of rules and precepts. He does not so much legislate as reason. He does indeed decide against divorce and discourage separation. The coming of the Lord was so momentarily expected that it was hardly worth while to marry or to separate. The matter of buying meat offered to idols he discusses with great vigor. He touches upon the claim of the party of "knowledge" of the right to buy their meat where they please, and then diverges sharply from the subject to tell of his own experience in giving up his rights because by so doing he could do a greater service for the Kingdom of God. He had found that there was sometimes a better use to be made of a right than to insist upon it, and that was to waive it for the sake of the greater service one could render by so doing. This digression from the argument gives us a vivid glimpse of the mind of Paul and shows something of what his missionary service had cost him personally.

The question of where the Corinthians should buy their meat was in itself an unimportant, even an insignificant matter, little calculated to rouse a teacher to any great heights of enthusiasm or eloquence. Yet Paul rose to just such heights in dealing with it, and it led him to develop two great ideals of social conduct which have never been outmoded or surpassed. For one thing, there is sometimes a better use to be made of a right than to insist upon it. In his own case, his whole usefulness to the Kingdom of God had hinged upon his renunciation of rights unquestionably his, to peace, home, tranquillity, security, respect, instead of which he had chosen these continual homeless wanderings, lonely, perilous, insecure, painful, even shameful, for the sake of the greater work he could do for the Kingdom of God. In this discovery Paul had struck to the basis of all social progress, which is made by the voluntary renunciation of individual natural rights to secure a larger social good. The general agreement in a country as to which side of the road to drive on is a familiar illustration, but the whole world is now interested in the application of this principle on the largest scale, in international relations. Nothing could better show the extraordinary vigor of

Paul's mind than his arrival at this tremendous truth from so trivial a starting point as the question of where the Corinthians should buy their meat.

Even this did not exhaust his thought upon the subject. For he perceived that even though the party of "knowledge" at Corinth, which had no scruple about buying meat at temple markets, knew that idols were nothing and the meat sacrificed to them was uninjured, yet the mere fact that frequenting them hurt the consciences of their Christian brothers should be enough to deter them from doing so. If what he ate made his brother fall, Paul for his part would never eat meat again, for certainly he was not going to make his brother fall. This is a point at which good morals and good manners seem to merge, and we hardly know which is involved. Certainly if his argument about the renunciation of rights shows Paul as a great thinker, his resolution not to hurt his brother's conscience reveals him as a great gentleman.

The Corinthians' questions about how women were to appear in Christian meetings, Paul dealt with from his inherited Jewish point of view. Jewish women did not form part of the synagogue's congregation, which consisted of men and boys. Paul and the Christians of Corinth went a long way when they admitted women freely to their meetings. But as to what they should wear at such public gatherings, Paul's Jewish upbringing left him in no doubt. They must wear veils, not on their faces but on their heads and shoulders. It would be disgraceful not to do so. Even here he does not legislate for them; he appeals to the Corinthians' native sense of propriety in support of this view. His unwillingness to have women speak in meeting was likewise a heritage from Judaism, but their inquiries could be addressed to their husbands at home, and if the husband chose he might bring such questions into public discussion.

The matter of ecstatic speaking and its bad effects upon the Corinthians' meetings might seem to give little promise of rich and fruitful religious treatment, but Paul found in it the opportunity of his life. For he showed the Corinthians that the solution of it was love, the Christian mutual consideration which thought first and always of the happiness and advantage of one's neighbors and companions. It was this matter of ecstatic speaking that led him to write the immortal thirteenth chapter of First Corinthians, on the supreme place and worth of love. The Corinthians thought ecstatic speaking was a gift, a spiritual endowment. But love is a gift too, and the greatest gift of all. It is the supreme gift of the Spirit, the loftiest Christian endowment. If in the ninth chapter he showed the way to social progress, in the thirteenth he disclosed to the Corinthians the grace of Christian courtesy, one of the great endowments of the Early Church, and depicted it in bold, vigorous strokes, every one of which is unforgettable. In the presence of this searching, moving, winning description of Christian love, it is hard to realize that what called it forth was the selfish insistence of a few Corinthians upon babbling in meeting.

But to Paul it was not small. For it imperiled the usefulness and dignity of the Corinthian church meetings, upon which so much depended. So he did not hesitate to spend himself and all he had to give upon the problem, and once more as with the question of where the Corinthians should do their marketing, he leads them to a great principle which covered the ecstatic speaking and a thousand times more, and still offers the noblest ideal of Christian behavior.

For the figure of Paul himself it means much too, for here was a man faced by problems of marketing and bad manners who does not think himself above them or dismiss them impatiently as unworthy of his serious attention. On the other hand, he thinks them through to solutions so sound and deep that the centuries have not outgrown them but rather have seen more and more in them with the passing years. So democratic a thinker was Paul.

A distinguished American philosopher a few years ago advanced the view that of Paul's great three, faith, hope and love, the greatest after all was really hope.[3] And Paul was far from unmindful of the place of hope in human experience. Whether Stephanas and his companions had asked him to do so, we do not know, but the last great note Paul was to strike in this most loved and famed of his letters was the note of hope, the Christian hope, of reunion, revival, resurrection, immortality. Paul viewed it as a real personal individual experience—a glorious prospect which robbed death of all its terrors and even made it something to be desired and welcomed. His view of it was strongly colored by the Pharisaic doctrine of bodily resurrection, and certainly no Pharisee had ever contended for it half as well as Paul did now, to the Corinthians. His magnificent argument rises in the end into a pæan. When in the splendid oratorio "The Messiah," the Resurrection music is so stirringly marshaled by the trumpets, it is Paul for a moment who is directing the orchestra:

"For the trumpet shall sound,
  And the dead shall be raised incorruptible,
  And we shall be changed."

Such was the letter that Stephanas and his party carried
back across the Ægean to Corinth and read at the next
meeting of the church there. How did Paul produce it? He
dictated it to some professional shorthand writer at Ephesus,
who could take his dictation, which must have been rapid,
to judge by the swiftly moving style he employed. Paul
may have used rough notes in his own hand to guide the
organization of what he wished to say, and the letter from
the Corinthians was before him. But in general, the letter
doubtless reflects his own familiar, extempore style of
preaching. It was very much in this way that he spoke in
the synagogue or the lecture hall of Tyrannus or before
the house congregations of Ephesus.

From the scribe's shorthand notes the letter would be
written up by him on a roll of papyrus about nine inches
wide and probably nine feet long, about one-third the maximum length of an ordinary Greek book, such as the Gospel of Matthew or of Luke, or The Acts of the Apostles.
This made a long letter for ancient or modern times, and
shows how prodigally Paul spent his powers upon preaching, teaching and correspondence. Few ancients and few
moderns have ever written so long a letter, and no other
ancient or modern has ever written so great a letter.

CHAPTER XIII 🙚 CONTROVERSY WITH CORINTH

AS PAUL writes First Corinthians his two years of preaching in the lecture hall of Tyrannus in Ephesus are drawing to a close and he is full of plans to visit Corinth. He hopes they will complete their gift of money for the Christian poor of Jerusalem so that he can take it with him when he goes on to the east. First he must go to Macedonia, but when he reaches Corinth he will make a long stay, and perhaps spend the winter before going to Jerusalem. For the present, however, the work in Ephesus is going so well that he must remain there at least until the harvest festival, toward the end of May. But much was to happen to interfere with these plans.

For I Corinthians had not had the effect upon the Corinthian cliques and factions that Paul had intended and hoped. Something about that great letter had deeply offended the Corinthians. Perhaps it was the stern rebuke with which the letter opened, or perhaps it was the importance Paul had attached to what Chloe's people had told him about the misdeeds of the Corinthians, their factions, lawsuits, immoralities and revels. At any rate so far from giving up their division into factions they had intensified it and were now forming one large Christ party in opposition to Paul. It was evident that some energetic and plausible person at Corinth was making it his business to crystallize this momentary resentment against Paul into organized opposition.

News of this soon made its way across the Ægean to Ephesus and greatly distressed Paul. Corinth was the first city in his missionary campaigns in which he had really had time enough to do his work, and this was the result! It was a bitter humiliation to him, and dependent as he was to a great extent upon his personal relationships, it reduced him almost to despair. He wrote of it afterwards to the Corinthians: "I do not want you, brothers, to misunderstand the distress I experienced in Asia, for I was so utterly and unendurably crushed, that I actually despaired of life itself. Why, I felt in my heart that the end must be death. That was to keep me from relying on myself instead of on God, who can even raise the dead. So deadly was the peril from which he saved me, as he will save me again!" Only the breaking up of what he had supposed established personal relationships could have caused Paul such distress as he here describes. A mere imprisonment, or even danger of death, would not have given him such anguish of spirit as this. He knew well enough that "stone walls do not a prison make, nor iron bars a cage." It would have taken more than another prison experience to shatter Paul's morale as it evidently was shattered at Ephesus. It was not any danger from the Ephesian mob or the city authorities there that had routed Paul. It was the thought that his old friends were going back on him and were his friends no longer; that his work at Corinth had collapsed at least as far as he was concerned, since the Corinthians had disowned him as a Christian leader.

Paul had done his utmost at Corinth. Getting employment at Aquila's shop, he had relieved the Corinthians of any financial responsibility for him, leaving them only the rent of the lecture hall to provide. He had stood up undismayed against the persistent attacks of the Jews there and had succeeded in staying on in Corinth until the church there had really won its way to a vigorous existence, and the ability to stand alone, as far as he was concerned. Now, just when he was absorbed in laying similar foundations in Ephesus, comes the news of this strange captious disaffection on the part of the Corinthians.

Paul's sharp criticism of them in his letter was not the only thing that had offended the Corinthians. A change in Paul's travel plans also annoyed them and gave them a ground for finding fault with him. He had written them that he was going from Ephesus to Macedonia, and then coming to see them, but he had changed this plan and resolved to come first to them on his way to Macedonia and then come back to them again after his visit there. Even this he had failed to carry out, thus giving a new grievance to his Corinthian critics, who declared him vacillating and unable to make up his mind. He was humble enough when he was in Corinth, they grumbled, and were bold only when he was at a safe distance. They charged him with worldly motives and with boasting of his authority over them. His letters, they admitted, were impressive, but his personal appearance was insignificant and as a speaker he amounted to nothing. While he never accepted money from them, he let other churches, like the Philippians, pay him while he was preaching to the Corinthians, and while refusing their money himself, he let his agents like Titus accept it. And after all, what proof of Christ's working through him had he ever really shown?

Paul's distress and indignation over these faultfindings stirred him to proceed at once to Corinth to confront his critics before the whole church and show himself in his true colors. But reflection showed him how painful this would be. It could be no very happy visit to arrive in Corinth as an unwanted guest. What pleasure could there be in that for them or for himself? He postpones his visit and writes a letter, which has come down to us appended to a subsequent letter to Corinth, in what we know as II Corinthians. The extraordinary incongruity of the two parts of II Corinthians, chapters 1–9 and chapters 10–13, which strikes every careful reader, is thus explained.

He plunges at once into the heart of the situation. He would appeal to them personally, by the gentleness and forbearance of Christ, yet he knows what they are saying, that he is humble enough when face to face with them and bold only when he is far away! They may yet find out how bold he can be when face to face! He runs over the list of their faultfindings and charges: his worldly motives, his boastfulness, his inferiority as a speaker, his independent financial policy, making them inferior to the Philippians.

If the boasts of his rivals in Corinth have so impressed them, let him have his boast too, foolish as it is to do so. Whatever anyone else dares to boast of, he will boast of too!

"If they are Hebrews, so am I! If they are Israelites, so am I! If they are descended from Abraham, so am I! If they are Christian workers—I am talking like a madman!—I am a better one! with far greater labors, far more imprisonments, vastly worse beatings, and in frequent danger of death. Five times I have been given one less than forty lashes, by the Jews. I have been beaten three times by the Romans, I have been stoned once, I have been shipwrecked three times, a night and a day I have been adrift at sea; with my frequent journeys, in danger from rivers, danger from robbers, danger from my own people, danger from the heathen, danger in the city, danger in the desert, danger at sea, danger from false brothers, through toil and hardship, through many a sleepless night, through hunger and thirst, often without food, and exposed to cold. And besides everything else, the thing that burdens me every day is my anxiety about all the churches. Who is weak without my being weak? Whose conscience is hurt without my being fired with indignation? If there must be boasting, I will boast of the things that show my weakness! The God and Father of the Lord Jesus Christ, he who is forever blessed, knows that I am telling the truth. When I was at Damascus, the governor under King Aretas had the city gates watched in order to catch me, but I was lowered in a basket from an opening in the wall, and got out of his clutches."

It would be difficult to match this extraordinary catalog of hardships anywhere in literature. But it was not written as literature. It was written in hot indignation at the Corinthians' depreciation of his work. And to that indignation we owe these amazing glimpses of what Paul went through in his missionary travels; the sheer physical obstacles he had surmounted. Very few of these experiences are reported or even reflected in The Acts, and the modern biographer is unable to place half of them in what he can learn of the movements of Paul. But only Paul himself knew the whole of it, and in his travels into and across Asia Minor, and his voyages about the Ægean and the eastern Mediterranean there was ample room for all he so vividly lists. What, indeed, could his rivals at Corinth offer in comparison even with these things that showed his weakness?

As for his visions and revelations, he will not speak of them; they are far too sacred for that. But he has been so privileged in such experiences that a bitter physical affliction has been sent upon him (perhaps his recurrent malaria), to keep him from too great elation. So he is perfectly willing to boast of all his weakness. He is pleased with weaknesses, insults, hardships, persecutions and difficulties, when they are endured for Christ's sake, for it is when he is weak that he is really strong.

As for this foolish boasting, the Corinthians have driven him to it, when they ought to have been expressing their approval of him. The facts show that he is not in the least inferior to their new self-styled apostles, though they may think him nobody! The only basis for their jealousy of his other churches is that he let them give him money, when he would not take it from the Corinthians—a strange ground of envy, truly, which they must try to forgive! But he has never wanted their money; children are not supposed to lay up money for their parents but parents for their children, and he is ready to spend all he has and all he is for them. Will they love him the less for this? As for Titus, he has never made any money out of them, any more than Paul has, but has closely followed Paul's example.

What he most fears is that when he comes to see them he will find quarreling, jealousy, ill feeling, slander and disorder rampant among them, and graver immorality unrepented of. They must examine and test themselves before he comes, and he prays that they may stand the test, for he wants to find all well at Corinth when he comes. He will be glad to be weak, if they are strong! For his authority is given him to build them up, not to pull them down.

There are times in the lives of many of us when it seems necessary to write a letter that will either make or break the situation. Such was the letter Paul now sent to the Corinthians. It was, he felt, a time to speak his mind, fully and forcibly, showing them the mistakenness of their attitude to him and yet declaring his unshaken affection for them. He sent it from Ephesus by the hand of a new comrade and lieutenant in his mission, the mysterious Titus, who is never mentioned in The Acts. It was a difficult and responsible errand, for the first effect of the letter might be to intensify the Corinthians' opposition to Paul, and it would be the business of Titus to reinforce the letter with efforts of his own, to reason with the Corinthians, and bring them to their proper senses, in their attitude to Paul.

Titus has already appeared upon the scene as the Greek convert who accompanied Paul from Antioch to the Jerusalem conference, and there became the representative instance of Greek freedom, since Paul persuaded the Jerusalem pillar-apostles that it was not necessary for him to accept circumcision. He was with Paul in Corinth, assisting him in his mission there, and faithfully following his policy of financial independence of the Corinthians. He now becomes the bearer of Paul's stern letter to Corinth, and as Paul is bringing his long period of work at Ephesus to a close, they arrange to meet at Troas, from which port they can go on together to Macedonia. About the same time, two other assistants of his, Timothy and Erastus, were despatched to Macedonia, where they were all to reassemble in a few weeks. After visiting the Macedonian churches at Philippi and Thessalonica, Paul intended to sail down to Corinth and then proceed to Jerusalem with the collection which he had been organizing among his western churches for the benefit of the Christian poor of the mother church.

Paul's work in Ephesus had met with extraordinary success. We have seen how the gospel was spreading from Ephesus into a whole series of outlying cities of Asia, and in Ephesus itself it was making a deep impression. One notable effect had been its impact upon the practices of magic, which in the middle of the first century were at their worst in the empire. Its devotees believed that by the use of certain formulas and incantations they could control events and destinies, cast out demons and dispel diseases. Followers of magic built largely on the knowledge of certain names and formulas, the possession of which gave them these powers. There had arisen a great number of these magical writings, which had a very substantial money value. Ephesus was famous for such texts, which in the ancient world sometimes went by the name of *Ephesia Grammata*, "Ephesian Writings." But such was the enlightening effect of Paul's preaching in Ephesus that great numbers of people realized the folly and wickedness of magical arts, and rather than leave such formulas where others might be misled by them, chose to destroy them in a great public spectacle. It was estimated that magical books worth fifty thousand drachmas, or at least ten thousand dollars, were thus destroyed. The Greek papyri, preserved mostly in Egypt, include numerous short pieces of this kind, besides one commanding collection of such formulas in the great magical papyrus in Paris.[1] Paul's preaching in Ephesus was at war with superstition, though later generations often sought to blend Christian as well as Jewish faith with such magical arts.

Paul's plans for leaving Ephesus were made and his rendezvous with Titus at Troas agreed upon, and Titus dispatched to Corinth with the heated letter already described, when a riot in the city occurred that probably hastened Paul's departure. Ephesus and the temple of Artemis there were constantly visited by pilgrims from all that part of the Greco-Roman world, and many of them made a point of buying a statuette of the famous image of the goddess that was preserved in the temple. Artemis of Ephesus was not at all the handsome athletic huntress of Greek mythology, but a half-Oriental, many-breasted figure symbolic of fertility. The making of these statuettes in pottery or metal for the tourist and pilgrim market was a considerable industry in Ephesus, but Paul's work there had had the effect of diminishing the demand for such idolatrous souvenirs. A silversmith named Demetrius who produced silver figures of Artemis for the richer visitors to buy and take home had felt this most keenly, and he assembled the workmen of his own and kindred trades to protest and start a movement against Paul and his work, as threatening not only their business but the prestige of Artemis and her famous shrine, a magnificent structure said to have been four times the size of the Parthenon, but a center of religious prostitution. The prospect of the decline of their industry and of the worship of their goddess roused these men to fury, and a riot ensued. The populace, stirred by the rumor that their local worship was in danger, rushed to the great theater, dragging with them two of Paul's traveling companions from Macedonia, Gaius and Aristarchus. Paul would have gone to their aid, but he was prevented not only by the Christian brothers but by some of the religious authorities who were his friends. The crowd blamed the Jews as well as Paul for what was happening, and the Jews tried to get a hearing for one of their number named Alexander, to defend them before the crowd in the great theater. They refused to listen, however, setting up instead a great outcry of cheering for Artemis. After two hours of this, the city recorder succeeded in quieting them, absolving the men they had seized from any blame, and referring the mob to the courts if they had a complaint to bring against anyone.

While Paul and his missionary companions escaped from this extraordinary mob scene unharmed, it plainly hastened his departure from Ephesus, and he never returned to the city. But his work there was perhaps in some respects the most fruitful and far-reaching of his whole career, for a generation later it was the church at Ephesus that collected and published his letters; that church was the home of the writer of the Revelation; there the Gospel of Luke and The Acts of the Apostles were written, and fifty years after Paul's work there it gave the world the Gospel of John and then collected and published the four Gospels. No church of the first century made a greater contribution to enduring Christianity than the one Paul founded in Ephesus. It was his last foundation, and his greatest.

CHAPTER XIV ✢ RECONCILIATION WITH CORINTH

FROM EPHESUS Paul made his way northward to Troas. He had written the Corinthians that he meant to stay in Ephesus until Pentecost, the time of the harvest festival in Palestine, but his departure may have been hastened by the anti-Jewish riot in which he had been involved and for which he was indirectly responsible. In Corinth it was Jewish hostility to his work that had flared up just before he left that city; in Ephesus it was anti-Jewish feeling that had risen against him. Whichever way the flood of Semitic or anti-Semitic feeling moved, he seemed to be involved in it. Worse still, the Corinthians' attack upon him had given his sensibilities what was almost a mortal wound. Sensitive and affectionate where his churches were concerned, he had felt it as a deathblow, a crushing disaster, which seemed to bring all his hopes to an end. He felt toward these young churches like a father or a mother, all affection and devotion, full of the tenderest concern. To have them turn from him in distrust and suspicion, even contempt, was too bitter to be borne. It filled him with despair, as no other experience could possibly have done.[1]

At Troas Paul found a promising opening for a Christian mission, but he had no heart to undertake it. What was the use of founding new churches, with his old ones crumbling beneath him? Worst of all, Titus did not appear to keep his appointment with Paul. Paul's mind could not rest; he bade his friends good-by and sailed for Macedonia. Even there he got no relief. There was trouble at every turn, fighting without and fear within. Where was Titus? What could be the meaning of his prolonged absence? Paul knew just how long the voyages involved would take, from Ephesus to Corinth, from Corinth to Thessalonica, or Philippi. A week should have been enough to deliver the letter, have it read to the congregation, and observe the reaction to it. Surely Titus could tell whether the Corinthians were moved by it to repudiate their new leaders and return to Paul! He could not understand what had happened to cause this delay. It could only mean that the letter had failed to produce the effect he so much desired.

When he was at his wits' end with anxiety and foreboding, Titus arrived. His report was favorable; the Corinthians had renounced the ringleader who had fomented the revolt against Paul and were now whole-heartedly back of Paul again. They had come over to his side. They recognize his great services to them, they are sorry for what they have done, they are indignant at the man who had led them into defiance of Paul and are directing all their wrath and vengeance upon him.

The Corinthians have, in fact, turned completely around. They are now wholly on Paul's side. They are eager to see him and can hardly wait for him to appear in person at Corinth. All Paul had ever said to Titus in praise of them had come true. Now they are all eagerness to clear themselves and to regain his confidence and approval. Paul is only afraid that in this strong revulsion of feeling they may go too far in punishing the man who has been chiefly responsible for their revolt against him; they must not now drive him, in his turn, to discouragement and despair.

Titus, it seemed, had supplemented the effect of the letter by his own efforts, and this had carried the day. It was a cause of no little importance that he had to plead, for not only Paul's happiness but the welfare and future of the Corinthian church hung in the balance. To refuse I Corinthians with its noble Christian ideals and hopes would have substituted an inferior kind of religion, of little use to the Corinthians or any others. And to have allowed I Corinthians to perish, as it would have done, had they persisted in their revolt, would have cost the world an incomparable piece of religious literature. It was to keep the new religion on a high plane, above any other in the ancient world, that Paul was straining every nerve. There were already plenty of faiths of lower orders, with base motives, lower morals and degrading practices. The ancient world was full of them. Some of them reveled in sex, some in intoxication, some in sensuous experience. They had their priests and prophets, too often venal and mercenary. Even Judaism had to choose between a selfish, worldly priesthood on the one hand and a proud, self-satisfied and exclusive faction on the other. Paul had found a higher path, and to it he had introduced the Corinthians. They must not lose it. He was immensely relieved to learn from Titus that they had not done so.

Of course, Paul could not wait until he should reach Corinth to express his relief and pleasure over all this. Wherever he was when Titus reached him, either at Philippi or Thessalonica, he wrote the Corinthians a letter, the fourth in his remarkable correspondence with them, preserved to us in

II Cor., chapters 1 to 9. He could not refrain from giving expression to the comfort and satisfaction Titus' news had brought him.

Paul begins with a great cry of thanksgiving: "Blessed be the God and Father of our Lord Jesus Christ, the merciful Father, and the God always ready to comfort!" This note of comfort he strikes again and again. Nine times in his first paragraph after the salutation he uses the word and comes back to it again toward the end of the letter. He recalls his bitter experience of anxiety and despair over their misunderstanding, and now reviews the points of difference between them in a gentler tone. He explains and even apologizes for the severity of his recent letter. "For I was in great trouble and distress of mind when I wrote you, and I shed many tears as I did it," he assures them. He begs them to forgive the man who has headed the revolt against him, and comfort him, or he may be overwhelmed by his remorse. Paul has forgiven the man, and they must do so too.

The basis of the trouble at Corinth had been a serious misunderstanding of Paul's motives and methods as a missionary, and this Paul now seeks to set right by a full statement on the subject. What could be of greater value for the understanding of the Early Church than such a statement of missionary methods and motives from the leading missionary of the first century? It is to this matter that Paul devotes most of this fourth letter to Corinth, II Cor. 2:12 to 6:10.

He is like one of those censer bearers who in ancient processions, when the proconsul rode in state up to the amphitheater, fumigated and perfumed the ill-smelling streets before and around him. In God's triumphal procession Paul is such a functionary, spreading the perfume of the knowledge of him everywhere. He is no peddler of God's message. He disowns disgraceful, underhanded ways. He refuses to use cunning or tamper with God's message. It is by the open statement of the truth that he would commend himself to every human conscience in the sight of God. It is not himself but Christ that he is proclaiming as Lord. Christ's love controls him. Through Christ, God has reconciled the world to himself, and he has intrusted Paul with the message of this reconciliation.

In a gentler spirit he reviews the long catalog of hardships he had given with such passion in his previous letter and describes the attitude of sincerity, patience, kindness and love which he maintains. This time, certainly, he has kept nothing back, but has spoken frankly, fully, and from the depths of his heart. They must meet him in a similar attitude. They must open their hearts to him, and he knows they will. His confidence in them is completely restored, he is proud of them again, he is fully comforted and overjoyed. Titus shares his satisfaction. He had told Titus what to expect of them, and they have faithfully fulfilled his expectations.

The time was approaching when Paul's long-planned gift from his Greek churches of the west to the needy brethren in Jerusalem must be completed and sent on to the church there and, in closing his letter, Paul turns to that matter. The Macedonian churches have been doing their part manfully and he knows the Corinthians will too. They had been the first to do anything about this collection or to take any interest in it. Indeed, he has been telling the Macedonian brethren how well they had been doing. It would seem that Corinthian subscriptions had been made, and he now wishes them to be paid so that there may be no delay in winding up the whole matter. The men who carried his letter to Corinth have his instructions to arrange for the paying in of the gift which they had promised, so as to have it ready. One of his agents is clearly Titus. The other is apparently his brother; certainly he is famous in all the churches for preaching the gospel. A third, a man of proved devotion to the cause and to them, accompanies them.

In these chapters Paul appears as a money raiser, and what a money raiser he was! The considerations he appealed to, the very words he used are still on our lips today, after nineteen hundred years. "The Lord Jesus himself, though he was rich, for your sake became poor, in order that by his poverty you might become rich." "If a man is willing to give, the value of his gift is in its proportion to what he has, not to what he has not." "The man who sows sparingly will reap sparingly." "God loves a cheerful giver." Years before, when the leaders of the Jerusalem church had pledged Paul and Barnabas their coöperation, they had asked them to remember the Jerusalem poor, and it was the promise he seems to have made at that time that he was now seeking to keep. But he sees in it much more than simply feeding some of the Jerusalem believers; what he hopes is that this gift will satisfy the Jerusalem brethren that the Greek Christians really have a sense of brotherhood for them. It will be a tie between these widely separated Christian groups and contribute to the unity of the church.

In this matter of the collection Paul appears as an organizer and administrator. He had evidently promised the Jerusalem leaders such financial help. He has been urging it in person both in Macedonia and in Greece. He pursues the subject in his letters, and he sends his representatives, Titus and the others, on ahead so that the matter may be well advanced in Corinth when he reaches there a few weeks later. The churches of Galatia and of Asia were also included in the plan, which thus made contact with two continents and spread over more than two years. It shows Paul as a humanitarian of energy and vision, with the larger concern for a united Christianity underlying it all.

If I Corinthians enables us to look into the mind of Paul, II Corinthians lets us look into his very heart, and we perceive that he was not only a man of great intellectual power but a man with a great emotional nature, frank, impulsive and sensitive, capable of deep feeling, of anxiety and grief, and of devotion and affection as well, and a man not afraid to express the whole range of such emotions, when occasion demanded it. Second Corinthians is, in fact, nothing less than a self-portrait of Paul.

CHAPTER XV ❧ LOOKING WESTWARD

PAUL'S VISITS to Philippi and Thessalonica were probably happy ones. His understanding with these Macedonian churches was generally good, his friends in Philippi being especially generous and loyal. He spent some anxious hours among them on this visit but it was Corinth that had caused his anxiety, and now that was removed. He prepared to follow his committee down the Ægean to Corinth.[1] There he spent three months with his reconciled Corinthians, completing the Jerusalem fund and planning its conveyance to Jerusalem.

One of Paul's first acts after reaching Corinth was to provide a Christian woman of the church at Cenchreae, the harbor on the Ægean side of Corinth, with a letter of introduction to the church at Ephesus. She was a helper or deaconess in her church, and whatever her errand in Ephesus, such a letter would assure her of being looked after and welcomed there. Ancient inns were notoriously of bad reputation; a Christian woman traveling alone could not be expected to stop in them, and her fellow Christians in Ephesus would take her to their homes, at least until she found a place to live. Such mutual hospitality was already the common practice in the Early Church.

Since leaving Ephesus a few weeks before, Paul has visited the churches of Troas, Philippi, Thessalonica, Berea and Corinth, and so he can say to the Christians at Ephesus,

"All the churches of Christ wish to be remembered to you." His only admonition to the church at Ephesus is a brief warning against people who try to introduce divisions among them. Everywhere among the churches he has found news of the progress of the church at Ephesus, and he is very happy about it himself. He sends greetings to a long list of Christians, men and women, twenty-four in all, besides the mother of Rufus and the sister of Nereus, the households of Aristobulus and Narcissus, the church that meets in the house of Prisca and Aquila and those who meet with Asyncritus, Phlegon, Hermes, Patrobas and Hermas. A third group meets with Philologus and Julia, Nereus and his sister and Olympas, unless we are to understand that three more groups are meant, one meeting with Philologus and Julia, another with Nereus and his sister, and a third with Olympas. There were evidently at least three groups or meetings within the Ephesian church, and possibly five, which is not at all improbable after Paul had worked there almost three years.[2]

Empire-conscious as he certainly was, Paul at Corinth overlooked the whole field of world-wide missions. He was the first statesman missionary. The importance of Rome itself in the missionary program did not escape him. Christianity had already reached the great capital of the empire, through unknown hands. Roman visitors to Jerusalem or to Antioch, travelers on Mediterranean vessels who had heard the gospel from the lips of fellow travelers, chance lodgers meeting believers at wayside khans on the Roman highways, Christian workmen moving from the east to look for jobs in Rome, slaves, soldiers, freedmen, passing along the arteries of the empire—these and others like them had brought the gospel to the heart of the Roman world and established it there. But beyond lay the western provinces of Gaul, Africa and Spain, and Paul's mind was already turning to the farthest of them, Spain, as a new field for his pioneering spirit.

Paul's interest in Spain shows how well informed he was of what was going on in the western provinces. For under Augustus and Tiberius, Spain had probably been developing faster than any other part of the empire. It had been colonized by Roman veterans and for half a century Roman engineers had been dotting it with temples, baths, theaters, aqueducts and bridges and veining it with roads. Paul must have known of Greek populations there ready for the gospel message. Certainly, even as he wrote to the Romans of his interest in Spain, the writing of Latin books was beginning to pass into the hands of men from that province, and for a century and a half Roman literature was to be chiefly the work of men like Seneca, Martial and Quintilian, who were born in Spain. It was the new world of the day, and somehow Paul had learned of its missionary possibilities and was already planning to take advantage of them. Massilia, the Greek Massalia (Marseilles), a Greek colony founded by the Phocæans about 600 B.C., had established a series of Greek trading posts along the Spanish coast, and the presence of a Greek element in the population of the coast cities, such as those we know as Rosas (Rhode), Ampurias (Emporiae), Barcelona, Tarragona, Valencia, Cartagena and Malaga, was insured by the prominence of Greeks as mariners and traders in the Roman world. Paul must have met some Greeks from Spain in his numerous voyages, and so have been led to the conviction that Spain should be the field of his next mission.

But first came Rome, a church he was resolved to reach and save from the false ideas of the gospel which had been such a peril in Galatia. And how easy it was for him now to get there! Corinth was the bridge between east and west. From Lecheum, the western port of the city, he could sail away through the Gulf of Corinth and across the Adriatic to Brundisium, and there find himself right on the Appian Way to Tarentum, Capua and Rome. In two weeks at the most he could be in Rome, for at Corinth he was really nearer to it, in terms of ancient travel, than he had been at any other point in his journeys. No doubt he already knew some of the Christians there and was stirred to help them. He had also a clear impression of the future importance of Rome in the spread of the Christian faith, an impression which history would far outrun. For every reason he was eager to visit Rome.

But his business in Corinth was to complete the collection and see to its transmission to Jerusalem. Paul attached great importance to it and to the effect it might have in welding together the widely scattered and very different parts of the Christian movement. For more than two years he had been bending his energies to this, and he was now occupied with helping the Corinthians to make a strong finish. He knew there was a church there, yet his mind is also busy with the Roman problem. What was going on at Rome? How immensely important to protect it from the sort of mistakes that had threatened the Galatians! He was strongly tempted to pay them a short visit just then. The money for Jerusalem could be sent by draft; such things were constantly done.

When at last the money was raised, and the committee named that was to take it, it was realized that half its effect would depend on how it was interpreted in Jerusalem, whether just as so much cash received or as a great symbol of fraternal fellowship from the Greek Christians of four provinces. A committee representing the churches of all four must accompany the gift, and no one, of course, could interpret it so well as the man who had planned and organized it, and in it was fulfilling a promise made long before to the Jerusalem leaders that he would remember the poor there. So Paul must head the committee going to Jerusalem.

Yet Paul could not escape the conviction that the Roman Christians needed some word from him to guide their thoughts and action in the practice of the new faith, and he had recourse once more to one of his characteristic procedures; he wrote them a letter. He did it out of the midst of the pressures of finishing the collection, preaching to the Corinthians, assembling his committee, and earning his living, but he did it without haste or precipitation. We must also think of it as in part the outgrowth of his recent active ministry in Ephesus and Macedonia and now again in Corinth. These thoughts had been taking shape in his mind during the months preceding as the things of deepest importance that he would like to say to the Roman Christians when he reached them. It reflected his own reading too, in a measure, for it shows acquaintance with a recent work of Egyptian Judaism, The Book of Wisdom, which had come out in Alexandria fifteen years before and had reached Paul probably not long before he wrote the letter to the Romans. Possibly Apollos brought it to his attention. He had come from Alexandria not long before and had been with Paul in Ephesus. It was a very small book, only half again as long as Paul's longest letter to Corinth, I Corinthians, but it seems fresh in Paul's mind when he writes to the Romans.

Paul had now had a long residence in two of the four greatest cities of the empire, Antioch and Ephesus. Only Rome and Alexandria were larger, and with his youth at Tarsus, Paul had come to know the life of the Roman world in some of its principal centers. It has often been pointed out that Paul was a man of cities. He was no rustic prophet like Amos or Micah, no hermit or anchorite, but a man who was most at home in a great city. He did not find God so much in storms and sunsets as in inner experience and human contacts. His figures, unlike those of Jesus, reflected principally urban life and relationships—the incense and libation in the Temple, the triumphal procession with its censer bearers, the races in the stadium, the boxer and the businessman.

Great thoughts were taking form in Paul's mind during those last busy weeks at Corinth, as he reflected on the young church at Rome and all that it might mean to the Christian movement in the years just ahead. His reading and his observations of life about him entered into his thinking, but only to form the materials for his deep reflection upon human life with its great needs and God's boundless mercy so ready to meet them. A vision came to him of divine compassion, forgiveness and love. It was for these that Christ had come into the world; this was the real meaning of the gospel. Over against the Law with its frightful background of curses [3] which drove sensitive, conscientious men like himself to sheer despair, Paul had come through Christ to see a merciful Father, more than ready to forgive and love his children.

The goal of religion, Paul felt, was uprightness, and a state of reconciliation and acceptance with God. But he was realistic enough to see about him a world of monstrous and degrading wickedness, brutal and violent without, and envious, treacherous and malicious within. The pagan world had turned away from the revelation of God in nature and descended to the corruptions and inanities of idolatry, and the worship of birds, beasts and reptiles. God in his turn has abandoned them to the gross and vicious existence they have chosen. Of the lofty ideal of religion, as conscious harmony with the living God, they have fallen far short. Yet miserable as their plight is they egg one another on to their destruction.

The Jewish world was no better. It was obstinate and impenitent, relying on its rite of circumcision and its religious heritage in the Law, and pronounced the rest of mankind sinners, even while it disobeyed the Law itself. Its pose of superior piety and its pride in its privileged relation to God has not prevented it from falling like the Greek world under the control of sin.

So Jews and Greeks alike are in the direst need of uprightness, but with no visible means of attaining it. But now God has through Christ revealed a way of becoming upright; it is the way of faith, for Jews and Greeks alike. Christ's death was a great gesture of reconciliation, a symbol of God's forgiveness, open to all who would accept it, whether Jews or Greeks. It was only when even Abraham had faith that he found his way to uprightness and God's approval. Christ's great sacrifice has consequences even more far-reaching than Adam's sin, which in Jewish thought brought guilt to all mankind, for Christ's death brings them forgiveness and life.

It all hinged upon faith, for faith revealed to men the divine forgiveness. But forgiveness is not forgiveness unless the person forgiven knows that he has done wrong and accepts the forgiveness. Only in that way can any forgiveness become real. Upon Paul had dawned the tremendous fact that God had forgiven the world. The death of Christ revealed it. It proved it, for Christ died for us while we were still sinners. Now with the gift of the Holy Spirit, God's love has flooded our hearts.

This magnificent amnesty, which was the heart of the gospel, had tremendous consequences for those who accepted it in faith. It delivered them from sin, it freed them from the Law, and it opened to them a new life, of freedom and uprightness, as sons of God, never to be separated from his love. Paul had made the greatest of all religious discoveries: he had found the river of the love of God, and his gospel was to make it known to all whom he could reach. Half a century later what he wrote to the Romans about it was nobly summarized in the greatest verse in the Gospel of John, in a sentence that is more Pauline than

Paul himself: "God loved the world so much that he gave his only Son, so that no one who believes in him should be lost, but that they should all have eternal life."

Many a time as Paul preached to Greek inquirers he must have been asked to explain the conduct of the Jewish people and tell why if Jesus was their Messiah they had refused to acknowledge him, and many a time the Roman Christians must have asked or been asked that question. Paul had an explanation of this. He still cherished the hope that ultimately the Jews would accept Christ, and as the problem was sure to rise in Rome, as it did everywhere else, he resolved to include it in his letter to Rome.

There had gradually been forming in Paul's mind a practical summary of Christian behavior—what the Christians' duties were, in the church, the state and society in general. They must obey the civil authorities and have for their brethren in the church a spirit of tolerance and patience. Who are they to criticize someone else's servant? "Let us not criticize one another any more." In writing this out for the Romans, Paul was offering a concise statement of practical Christian duties surpassed only in the Sermon on the Mount.

All this rich result of his experience and reflection Paul rolled into a letter, in those ninety days in Corinth, and when he set out with his committee from Cenchreae for Jerusalem, some faithful messenger left Corinth by its other port, Lecheum, for Brindisi and Rome. It was meant to safeguard the Roman church against perils Paul's other churches had already encountered, and it was also in a sense testamentary, for Paul was facing no small danger in going to Jerusalem, and if he never came back to the west, the Roman church would still possess in this letter his last will and testament, bequeathing to them this fullest statement of his gospel. It was not written under the pressure of any compelling crisis, and so it embodies Paul's idea of the gospel in a more constructive, proportioned fashion than Galatians, or I or II Corinthians, echoes and reminiscences of which appear here and there in its pages.

So like bread cast upon the waters, Paul lavished his great letters upon the small struggling church groups of his day, hoping for an immediate result, but little dreaming of all they would mean to later generations of believers. He was setting his face to go to Jerusalem, while his new letter, the most carefully planned and written of them all, was being carried west to Rome. When he sailed from Cenchreae, there were four letters from him lying about the church at Corinth, in the church chest or in the house of Gaius or in the hands of Stephanas or some other officer of the Corinthian church. Somebody there certainly prized the letters enough to keep them, and so started the stream of transmission that was to preserve them as a rich legacy for Christians ever after.

CHAPTER **XVI** ❧ TURNING EASTWARD

PAUL HAD reached a great decision. He would go to Jerusalem. When he gave up his plan to visit Rome and go on west to Spain, and turned eastward with the collection instead, he made a choice that was fateful and even fatal, for it was to cost him his liberty and finally his life. If he had decided differently and followed his impulse to go to Rome, and then to Spain, Christian history would have been different, perhaps very different. But before we regret his choice too much, we may remember that in that case we should have been without the letter to the Romans, and Christian literature would have suffered a major loss.

Paul now found himself sitting on a spring night on the deck of a ship in the harbor of Cenchreae, for soon after midnight she would sail. He had hoped to be sailing for Italy that night, but he had felt that he was only postponing his visit to Rome, and he was sending his Roman friends his letter instead. None of the Corinthians who were seeing him off realized it was the greatest letter ever written, or that this man was the greatest thinker of his day; perhaps at that moment the most important man in the world, and the one destined to have the most far-reaching influence. But they all knew that his interests reached out east and west, to help the people of Jerusalem and of Rome, and if possible to unite both Jews and Greeks in the service of the

Kingdom of God. So great a figure was the Jewish workman sitting on the deck of the ship that lay waiting for the early morning breeze.

Disappointed in his dream of turning westward to Rome and Spain, Paul had intended to take a ship bound directly for Syria, but something had happened at the last moment to alter his plans. A Jewish plot against him had come to his knowledge, and he had suddenly changed his sailing and shipped on a vessel bound for Macedonia. The Jews' hostility to him was doubtless due to their idea of him as a renegade and an enemy of Judaism, and his foes had thought that on a crowded pilgrim ship bound for the east in time for the Passover they could do what they liked with him without fear of detection. Jewish nationalism was beginning to run high just then, and within ten years it was to break out into open rebellion against the authority of the Roman Empire.

Upon Paul's arrival in the Macedonian cities of Thessalonica and Philippi, the full committee which was to carry the money that had been raised for Jerusalem was made up. Seven of them went on ahead to Troas; among them they represented three of the four provinces, the churches of which had joined in the collection. From Macedonia there were Sopater of Berea and Aristarchus and Secundus of Thessalonica; from Galatia there were Gaius of Derbe and Timothy of Lystra; from Asia there were Tychicus and Trophimus. The Jews were accustomed to large delegations bringing gifts of money to the Temple, especially at festivals. These men had probably been active in raising the fund they were carrying; perhaps some were among the principal contributors to it. Paul and Luke followed them five days later, sailing from Philippi after the days of unleavened bread, early in April. Luke added a third to the Macedonian delegation, probably representing Philippi. The absence of anyone from Corinth suggests that the Corinthians had fixed upon Paul himself as their representative.

The company spent a week at Troas, where a church had been formed. On the last night of their stay Paul preached long and earnestly to them; all through this journey there was an undercurrent of apprehension that he might never be able to return. It might be the last time he would address them, and he spoke till midnight. A young man named Eutychus, sitting at a window, went to sleep and fell out, from the third story. They picked him up for dead, but Paul took him in his arms and declared him still alive. Paul then went upstairs again and completed his address, and they all had the Lord's Supper together. Paul talked with the people until dawn and the ship with his delegates had sailed, but he had planned to go by land to Assos, some twenty-five miles south, and rejoin it there. He evidently wanted all the time possible with his new friends at Troas, where the year before he had thought of undertaking missionary work. Luke, the veteran traveler, records the day's runs; the first to Assos, on the south coast of the Troad, some forty miles; the next to Mitylene, about thirty-five; the third to Chios, about sixty miles; the fourth to Samos, some seventy miles; and the fifth, perhaps thirty miles, to Miletus. An ancient ship under the most favorable conditions could make a hundred and twenty-five miles in twenty-four hours, but these vessels were evidently coasters, which tied up at night at one of these numerous island ports and did principally a local business.

The temptation to stop at Ephesus was great, but Paul wished to reach Jerusalem by the harvest festival, or Pentecost, which fell seven weeks after the Passover, and at least two weeks had already passed, for he had not left Philippi until after the Passover. If it was hard to tear himself away from the brethren at Troas, it would be far more difficult to get away from Ephesus. He contented himself with asking the elders of the church there to come around to Miletus to meet him. It was only some thirty miles in a straight line, but more than twice that distance by land or sea.

It was a moving farewell, for a farewell it was. Paul spoke with foreboding of his coming visit to Jerusalem and declared his deep conviction that they would never see him again. He reviewed his blameless life among them and solemnly intrusted the church at Ephesus to their charge. At the end he knelt down and prayed with them. Weeping aloud, the elders kissed him good-by and then went with him to the ship, to see him off on the next stage of his journey.

Paul's old friend Luke, who had first guided him into Europe seven momentous years before, and had probably been active in the money-raising campaign in Philippi, noted the progress of the voyage with characteristic detail.[1] A straight run of some sixty miles brought them to Cos; then in a long day's run of perhaps eighty miles they made Rhodes, where enormous fragments of the colossal bronze statue of the sun-god, long before shattered by an earthquake, were still lying about the port. Another day's run of some seventy miles brought them to Patara, the harbor of the town of Xanthus in Lycia near the southwestern corner of Asia Minor. Here they transferred to a ship bound for Phœnicia, which struck southeast across the Mediterranean and, leaving Cyprus on her left, made for Tyre. Phœnician ships were still considered the best built and the best manned on the sea. They were now in scenes new to Luke and to most of the party. He was interested in the course they took, and in the sight of the mountains of Cyprus, visible to the east and north, on the port side. He knew that island as the scene of Paul's first missionary labors. This voyage, close to four hundred miles without a landing, must have taken at least four days, so that Paul landed at Tyre at the earliest on the eleventh day out from Troas.

At Tyre the apostle and his party spent a week, while the ship was unloading and perhaps taking on fresh cargo. They sought out the Christian group there and were entertained in their homes. Here was a group of believers in close touch with conditions in Jerusalem, and they pronounced them very serious. In the most solemn manner, they warned Paul not to set foot in that city. Their conviction that it would be extremely dangerous for him to show himself in Jerusalem simply confirmed his own apprehensions, which he had expressed to the Ephesian elders at Miletus, when he told them they would never see him again. But in Palestine he learned more of the disturbed state of things than he could have believed when he was five hundred miles away, in Macedonia or Greece.

Matters had been bad enough in Judea under the Roman procurator Cumanus, five or six years before. Riots and reprisals had then been the order of the day in Jerusalem. But for the last four years, since the banishment of Cumanus and the sending of the freedman Felix to Judea as procurator, matters had deteriorated rapidly. There had been bloody conflicts in Galilee and Samaria, and the Jewish population in general had gone over to the side of the Sicarii or Daggermen, who were the conspicuous figures in the revolt. The country was seething with rebellious feeling, which every now and then broke into open revolt. The arrival in Jerusalem of a leading Christian like Paul, who was known to be identified with the mission to the Greeks, might easily touch off another of these explosions, in which the Romans were more than likely to seize upon the innocent victim of the attack and punish him for it. Indeed, they had done just this on more than one occasion already in Palestine.

The welcome given Paul and his party by the church at Tyre was most cordial and generous. When the time came for them to sail, the Tyrian Christians with their families escorted them out of the town to the port and saw them on board the ship which was to take them farther south to Ptolemais, a short run of thirty miles. There again the party was welcomed by the local church, and spent a day with the brethren. Another short run of about thirty-five miles the next day brought their long voyage to an end at Cæsarea, the Roman headquarters for Palestine.

At Cæsarea, Philip the missionary made his home, with his four maiden daughters, who had the gift of prophecy.

He was one of the seven deacons appointed by the Jerusalem church years before to look after its business matters. Philip was the man whose casual meeting with an Ethiopian official on the road to Gaza a few years before had led to the Ethiopian's conversion and to the planting of the gospel in that distant country.

Paul's party remained in Cæsarea for some days, Paul and Luke being entertained in Philip's house. While they were there a Christian prophet named Agabus came down from Judea. He frankly declared that Paul would be imprisoned if he went up to Jerusalem and illustrated it in the graphic fashion of the old Hebrew prophets, by taking Paul's belt and tying his own hands and feet with it.

"This is the way," he said, "that the Jews at Jerusalem will bind the man who owns this belt, and will hand him over to the heathen!"

This was the third premonition that had met Paul on his journey, and it came with especial force since Agabus had just come from Judea and knew what was going on there. Evidently matters there were going from bad to worse, and there was every reason to believe Paul's presence would provoke violence. Here as at Tyre a few days before, the warning was given Paul as from the Holy Spirit itself, which makes it all the stranger that he paid no attention to it. Luke and his companions joined Philip and his family in imploring Paul not to go up to Jerusalem, but he declared his readiness to die there, if need be. His mind was made up. He was resolved to deliver this gift to the Jerusalem church and to make its meaning plain to them, as a symbol of the Christian brotherhood of the Greek churches of the west, whatever might befall him. Above all other considerations, he valued the unity of Greek and Jewish Christianity and was fully prepared to sacrifice himself if necessary to secure it. Perhaps like Jesus he felt that prophets should die in Jerusalem.[2]

It was two full days' journey to Jerusalem, and some of the brothers from Cæsarea escorted Paul and his eight companions to the home of a veteran disciple named Mnason, where they broke the journey and spent the night. Like Barnabas, Mnason was a man of Cyprus and lived at Antipatris or Joppa, halfway points between Cæsarea and Jerusalem. From his house the brothers from Cæsarea turned back the next morning to return home, while Paul and his party set out on the last stage of their long journey, the forty miles or so that would bring them to Jerusalem, a journey of eleven or twelve hours on horseback. It would be Paul's fifth visit, that we know of, to the city, but probably all his companions were approaching the Holy City for the first time. Anyone who has ridden into Jerusalem for the first time can imagine something of their emotions, as they came within the walls of the Holy City.

CHAPTER **XVII** 🕊 CRISIS AT JERUSALEM

THE JERUSALEM to which Paul now returned again after an absence of eight years was a very different place from the city he had known so well. Materially it was indeed little altered. The Temple still stood, set high on the eastern side of the city, looking across the Kidron Valley to the Mount of Olives. The frowning Roman fortress Antonia still faced it on its northern side. Herod's great palace, with its three famous towers of his construction, Hippicus, Phasaelus and Mariamne, still dominated the western front of the city. All in all, Jerusalem had never been more splendid.

But among the people all was changed. Some change Paul could see for himself, and much more he was soon informed of. The Jewish populace was in a highly inflammable mood. About the time of Paul's last visit, A.D. 48, the Emperor Claudius had sent Cumanus out as procurator, and the insolence and indecency of one of his soldiers at Passover time provoked a riot in the crowded city which was ruthlessly put down with great loss of life. The Sicarii, or Daggermen, who carried daggers under their cloaks, formed robber bands out in the country and robbed a Roman agent. One of the soldiers sent out to bring in the local villagers for examination tore up a copy of the Torah and burned it. A multitude of Jews proceeded to Cæsarea to demand satisfaction of Cumanus, who had the soldier executed. Some Galilean pilgrims passing through Samaria on their way to the Passover became involved in a fight with some villagers, and one pilgrim was slain. The Galileans rallied to the attack. Some leading men appealed to Cumanus to punish the murderer, but he put them off. The news reached Jerusalem, and a horde of pilgrims left the feast and set out for Samaria, where they killed the villagers and burned the villages. This roused Cumanus, and he sent soldiers from Cæsarea to the scene. They killed many of the Jewish horde and arrested others, but it required the entreaties of the Jewish authorities in Jerusalem to stay the fanatical violence of the pilgrims. Some of these irreconcilables joined the robber bands and the disorder spread over the country. The Samaritans protested to Quadratus, the legate of Syria, and the leaders of the Jews reached him at Tyre with their side of the case. Quadratus crucified the Jewish prisoners and executed eighteen other Jews who had been involved in the attack on the Samaritans. He sent Cumanus to Rome for trial before the Emperor Claudius, who took the side of the Jews, and put the leading Samaritans to death. Claudius also removed the procurator Cumanus from office and banished him, putting a freedman named Felix, the brother of his favorite, Pallas, in his place.

Felix captured the robber leader Eleazar and many of his band and put them to death. But the Sicarii became bolder and bolder. One of their first victims was the high priest Jonathan, and so many were killed after him that a hideous state of fear and suspicion ensued; men hardly knew friend from foe. Assassination was a daily occurrence. Political Messianists also contributed to the confusion, leading their followers off into the wilderness where the Roman authorities, suspecting revolt, pursued and destroyed them.

An Egyptian false prophet gathered an immense following estimated at thirty thousand men and appeared at their head on the Mount of Olives, with the intention of taking Jerusalem. But the Roman soldiers, aided by the people of the city, defeated them with great slaughter.

Such were the stories of disaster and disorder that were on men's tongues in Jerusalem when Paul reached the city. Young Josephus, soon to enter his novitiate as a prospective Essene, heard them and wrote them down long after in his *Wars of the Jews* as the preliminaries of the Jewish War, which was to break out ten years later.[1] The Christian leaders in Jerusalem knew these stories and more too, and there were anxious interviews between them and Paul. Paul had no wish to see his nation perish; as he had told the Romans just before he sailed for the east, he was profoundly concerned for their salvation, and he knew these assassins and gangsters were the worst enemies of Judaism. Modern readers of the story are constantly reminded of the desperate Palestine situation in our own times of which they read in the morning papers or heard over the radio. The Irgun Zvai Leumi and its doings recall those of the Jewish Zealots and Sicarii, the assassins and cutthroats of the last sad years of Jerusalem and Judaism.

Certainly Paul had no desire to do anything to excite or inflame the populace of Jerusalem. He must have viewed the whole situation with regret and apprehension. Himself a loyal citizen of the empire, he believed the Christian's duty to be loyalty and obedience. He was on the side of

law and order, as he plainly told the Christians at Rome.
Yet memories of Jesus' words of doom for the unrepentant
city were coming back to men's minds, and how he had
warned his followers when they saw the doom approaching
to make the greatest possible haste to flee from the city:
"A man on his housetop must not go down, to go into
the house or to get anything out of it, and a man in the field
must not turn back to get his coat." [2]

Still the Jerusalem Christians gave Paul and his companions a warm welcome. Paul made it his first business to
call upon James, the head of the Jerusalem church, and
present Luke, Timothy, Tychicus and the other Greek representatives to him. There in the presence of the elders of
the church the fund was turned over to the proper church
authorities, and Paul gave a full account of the progress
of the Greek mission since his last appearance before them,
eight years before.

They in turn told him of the growth of the Jewish
church in Judea and warned him that unfavorable reports
about him and what he taught were current among them.
These Jewish Christians evidently adhered to the traditional customs of Judaism, as to circumcision, foods and
the like, and they had heard that out in the west Paul was
teaching Jews to abandon such practices and live as the
Greeks did. This charge was undoubtedly true. It was the
unwillingness of Cephas and Barnabas at Antioch to follow
him in this course that Paul so rebuked in his letter to the
Galatians. On the other hand, he saw nothing wrong in
the Jewish Christians of Judea continuing their traditional
social practices. The Jerusalem leaders proposed that he

should join a group of four men who were just about to go through some Temple rituals such as Jewish Christians still followed. These man had undertaken a Nazirite vow, for a limited period, and had incurred some defilement, perhaps through touching a dead body, which called for a week of purification and sacrifice. Paul, they suggested, might pay for the four lambs and eight pigeons required for sacrifice and attend the men in their Temple appearances and rituals, which lasted a week and culminated in having their heads shaved and burning their hair on the altar. This would involve Paul's crossing the Court of the Gentiles and the Court of the Women, entering the Court of Israel, and finally approaching the altar of burnt offering itself. Paul had come to Jerusalem to do all in his power to hold the Jewish and Greek wings of the church together, and he readily agreed.

The ceremonies occupied a week and were almost over when some Jews from Ephesus caught sight of him in the Temple. They had seen him often before, in Ephesus, and regarded him as a renegade from Judaism and a man who spent his life undermining the Jewish Law which they so prized. They raised a loud outcry.

"Men of Israel, help!" they shouted. "This is the man who teaches everybody everywhere against our people and the Law and this place, and besides he has actually brought Greeks into the Temple and desecrated this sacred place."

They had seen and recognized the Ephesian Trophimus going about the city with Paul and had concluded that he proposed to smuggle him into the Temple, a deadly offense, as huge Greek inscriptions placed at all the entrances to the Court of the Women declared. In the highly inflammable state of the Jewish mind at the time, this cry raised by the Jews from Ephesus was like a trumpet call. It flashed through the Pentecost throngs about the Temple and down into the streets of the city. As if by magic, a crowd gathered. Paul was seized and hurried out of the Temple down the steps into the Court of the Gentiles. The Temple gates clanged shut behind the mob. The angry crowd, incensed by the rumor that he had been caught desecrating the Temple, was thronging about him and working itself into a murderous mood, when the watchful Roman sentries from the roofs of the Temple porticoes or from the Castle Antonia, which commanded the Temple at its northwest corner, observed the disturbance and called out the guard. Immediately the colonel of the regiment gathered some officers and men and came swiftly down the stairs that led from the Antonia right into the Court of the Gentiles.

At sight of the descending Romans the rabble gave up beating Paul and stood aside. The colonel, Claudius Lysias, came up and arrested him, as the manifest cause of the disturbance, had him chained to a couple of soldiers, one on each side, and then asked the bystanders what he had been doing. Some shouted one thing and some another, and as he could make nothing of their statements, he ordered Paul taken up to the castle. The mob, disappointed in its purpose to make an end of him, crowded about shouting "Kill him! Kill him," and pressing them so closely that Paul was carried off his feet as they mounted the stairs.

At the top of the stairs Paul got the colonel's attention for a moment.

"May I say something to you?" he asked.

The colonel was surprised.

"Do you know Greek?" he asked. "Aren't you the Egyptian who some time ago gathered four thousand of the Assassins and led them out into the wilderness?"

"I am a Jew," said Paul, "from Tarsus, in Cilicia, a citizen of no unimportant city. I beg you, let me speak to these people."

The colonel was a good deal surprised at the request. The mob was surging about the lower stairs; only the soldiery was keeping Paul out of their reach. From the top of the steps Paul and the Roman colonel looked down upon a scene of wild confusion in the corner of the Court of the Gentiles.

The colonel was accustomed to such popular outbursts over little or nothing as far as he could understand, but this man was hardly the ordinary ruffian usually at the bottom of these riots. He had the manner of a man of education and position and called himself a citizen of Tarsus. He decided to let him speak and see what he could do with these fanatics.

So from the top of the flight of stairs that led up from the court to the Castle Antonia, with the whole dazzling pile of Herod's Temple towering at his left, Paul raised his hand for silence.

"Brethren and fathers," he began, in their native Aramaic, "Listen to what I have to say in my defense."

Accustomed as he was to the ways of crowds, his first

words, calm and polite, and in their own speech, quieted them.

"I am a Jew," he went on, "and I was born in Tarsus in Cilicia, but brought up here in this city, and thoroughly educated in the Law of our forefathers under the teaching of Gamaliel." He went on to tell of his zeal for the Law, his persecution of the Christians, under orders from the high priest himself, his journey to Damascus with letters from the council to carry on his inquisition there; then as he approached the city, his vision, his conversion, his return to Jerusalem, and his commission to preach Christ to the heathen.

So far the crowd had heard him patiently, but at this point the suggestion of giving their precious hopes of national exaltation to the heathen whom they hated and despised revived all their rage. They began to roar, throwing handfuls of dust and even their clothes into the air. "Kill him!" they shouted. "Get him out of the world. Such a fellow mustn't be allowed to live!"

The colonel thereupon hurried Paul into safety in the barracks and gave orders to have him examined under the lash, to get the truth out of him as to what all the outcry was about. He left this to one of his junior officers and went his way. But as they were strapping Paul up as a preliminary to carrying out their orders, Paul said to the officer, "Is it legal to flog a Roman citizen, and that without giving him a trial?"

This brought matters to a sudden halt. The officer suspended operations and hurried off to find the colonel and report.

"What are you about?" he said. "This man is a Roman citizen."

This brought the colonel back to the scene. He began to look at Paul a little more closely.

"Tell me," he said to him, "are you a Roman citizen?"

"I am," said Paul.

Paul did not look like a rich man to the colonel.

"I had to pay a large sum for my citizenship," said the colonel.

"I am a citizen by birth," said Paul.

The men who had been about to flog Paul immediately disappeared, and the colonel was a little uneasy at what he had already done to a citizen of the empire. The extension of the citizenship to provincials had been one of the policies of the last emperor, Claudius; indeed one Roman satirist expressed fear that he would end by making all the provincials citizens, and only hoped he would at least leave a few noncitizens, as he said, "for seed." Lysias was probably a Greek, as his name suggests, who had acquired his citizenship under Claudius five or ten years before, when the wife and courtiers of that emperor got a steady income from selling the citizenship to moneyed people. Lysias' praenomen Claudius suggests that he had gained his citizenship under that emperor. He gave up the idea of flogging Paul, but held him for examination later.

So in a minor collision with the Jewish revolutionaries at Jerusalem, Paul's liberty came to an end, and with it all the great plans of wider missionary work he had in view. His active work was done. Only a few months before, he had summarized it in concluding his letter to the Romans, feeling even then that his work in the east was finished; he had "completed the preaching of the good news of Christ all the way from Jerusalem around to Illyricum" (Rom. 15:19). He himself clearly felt that he had concluded a great chapter in his missionary work; as he put it, there was no more work for him in that part of the world. But he could not know that it was definitely over, though he had his misgivings and forebodings (Rom. 15:31). Much indeed remained for him to do, but he was to do it as a prisoner of the Roman authorities, not as a free man, going wherever he pleased about the empire. It says much for his personal power that he still continued by his letters and his personal contacts to dominate and direct the Greek mission as he did. And from a personal standpoint, his story now takes on a new and increased dramatic interest.

CHAPTER **XVIII** 🙠 A PRISONER IN PALESTINE

PAUL HAD been arrested by the Roman colonel Claudius Lysias partly to put a stop to the riot, of which he was evidently the object, partly to protect him from the Jewish mob, and partly to examine him and find out whether or not he was wilfully a disturber of the peace. In order to get at the facts in the case and learn why the Jews were so hostile, Lysias called for a meeting of the Jewish council the next morning and took Paul before it. The council was composed of the leading members of the priesthood, who were Sadducees, and a larger number of members of the Pharisee party. It usually met in a room in the Court of Israel in the Temple. Confronted by this body, Paul lost no time in declaring that he had done what he regarded as his duty to God, in the course he had followed. At this the high priest Ananias ordered the men standing nearest to Paul to strike him on the mouth for such audacity. Paul replied with vigor.[1]

"God will strike you, you white-washed wall!" he cried, "Do you sit there to try me by the Law, and order them to strike me in violation of the Law?"

Paul's neighbors in the assembly rebuked him.

"Do you mean to insult God's high priest?" they demanded.

Paul immediately apologized.

"I did not know, brethren, that he was high priest; for

the Scripture says, 'You shall not say anything against any ruler of your people.' "

Paul had never been a member of the council, but his former membership in the Pharisaic party made him quick to observe the number of Pharisees present in the council; perhaps their well-known fondness for religious dress, amulets, long robes and long tassels, which they liked to wear not simply in prayer but on all occasions helped him to recognize them. He adroitly diverted the discussion to a well-known point of difference between Sadducees and Pharisees—the resurrection of the dead.

"Brethren," he cried, "I am a Pharisee, and the son of Pharisees! It is for my hope for the resurrection of the dead that I am on trial!"

It was true the Resurrection of Christ was central in Paul's Christian convictions, and in that respect and in some others his faith was much nearer the Pharisaic than the Sadducean belief. Some of the Pharisees got up and declared him innocent. In reality, his case involved far more than that, yet this apple of discord that he flung among them did in fact divide them so sharply that a violent dispute arose, and when the colonel heard of it, fearing they would kill Paul, he sent word down to have him brought back to the castle again.

Paul had now been in great personal danger on two successive days, but that night his courage was revived by a vision of Christ, standing at his side and saying, "Courage! For just as you have testified for me in Jerusalem, you must testify in Rome also."

Already the conviction was forming in Paul's mind that

his only way of escape from this Jerusalem situation would be by way of Rome.

He had a nephew in Jerusalem, his sister's son, who remained friendly to him and now did him a marked service. This young man must have had some contact with the Jewish underground, for he had learned that forty men, obviously Sicarii, had conspired to kill Paul and taken an oath not to eat or drink until they had done so. They were expecting the council to ask for a further hearing of his case and planned to take advantage of his coming down from the safety of the castle into the Court of the Gentiles, where they could attack him.

Paul's nephew immediately made his way to the castle and succeeded in reaching Paul and warning him of the plot. Paul called one of the officers to him and asked him to take his nephew to the colonel as he had something to tell him. The officer complied.

"The prisoner Paul," he told the colonel, "called me to him and asked me to bring this young man to you, as he has something to tell you."

The colonel had already begun to take Paul seriously. He took the young man aside and asked him what he had to tell him. Paul's nephew told him the whole story.

"The Jews," he said, "have agreed to ask you to bring Paul down to the council tomorrow, on the ground that you mean to have a fuller inquiry made into his case. But do not let them persuade you, for more than forty of them are lying in wait for him, and they have taken an oath not to eat or drink until they have killed him. They are all ready now and are only waiting to get your promise."

This lurid story did not appear to the colonel in the least improbable, and he acted on it immediately. He gave orders at once that Paul should be transferred to Cæsarea that very night under a strong guard. An escort of two hundred footmen, seventy mounted men, and two hundred spearmen was to set off at nine that night, to get him in safety to Felix, the procurator. The fact that Paul was a Roman citizen made Lysias anxious to get him into the hands of the procurator, and at a safe distance from the local insurrectionists. The size of the guard he was providing shows how unsettled the country was getting to be and to what lengths the guerillas who infested it might be expected to go. He sent the governor a letter, reporting that a Roman citizen named Paul had come into his custody and explaining why he was sending him to Felix for further hearings.

The distance to Cæsarea was some sixty miles, and Antipatris was a little more than halfway. The foot soldiers who made up the bulk of the escort saw the expedition well out of the danger zone, to Antipatris, and then dropped out to return to Jerusalem next day, leaving the cavalry to complete the journey to Cæsarea with Paul, who was there handed over to the custody of the governor, together with the letter from Claudius Lysias, the colonel at Jerusalem. Felix assured Paul that he would hear his case as soon as his accusers arrived, and had him kept in Herod's palace, which now served as the headquarters of the Roman governor of Palestine.

Five days later a delegation came down from the council in Jerusalem, headed by the high priest Ananias, and accompanied by an attorney, to present the case in legal fashion. Paul was brought in, and the attorney Tertullus presented his argument. He represented Paul as a leader of the Nazarene sect and a disturber of the peace among Jews all over the world. His most recent offense had been an effort made within the past week to desecrate the Temple at Jerusalem, but it had been thwarted by the Jews. The Jewish delegation supported his claims.

When Paul was given an opportunity to reply, he pointed out that he had gone up from Cæsarea to Jerusalem only twelve days before and had made no disturbance of any kind in the city or the Temple. He admitted that he belonged to what they considered a sect which believed in resurrection, but he declared that his conscience was clear. He also pointed out that the Jews from Asia who had made the charge against him should be present to testify, or that the Jews from Jerusalem should state what their council there had found wrong with him.

Felix knew something about the Christian movement and adjourned the hearing until Lysias the colonel should come down to Cæsarea. Ananias and his party returned to Jerusalem. There he perished miserably ten years later, in the beginning of the Jewish rebellion, being killed by a mob of revolutionists which attacked and burned his house.

So began Paul's two years of imprisonment in Cæsarea. He was kept in custody, but allowed some freedom, and his friends were permitted to come and look after him. No doubt he continued his correspondence with his churches as necessity arose, but action upon his case was deferred.

Paul seems to have made a strong impression upon everybody who came in contact with him, and even Felix felt that there was something extraordinary about him, for he had him called in on one occasion to explain his religious views before Felix and his wife Drusilla. This beautiful princess, then about nineteen years old, was the youngest daughter of Herod Agrippa I, who had been king of Palestine from A.D. 41 to 44. She was the younger sister of Herod Agrippa II. Agrippa I was the grandson of Herod the Great and Mariamne, so that Drusilla was a direct descendant of the Maccabean princes. Drusilla was only sixteen when she married the freedman Felix, then procurator of Judea, but she had previously been the wife of Aziz, king of Emesa, whom Felix, with the aid of a magician, had persuaded her to leave. Felix would send for Paul occasionally and listen to his teaching of uprightness, self-control and coming judgment. When it became too personal and alarming Felix would dismiss the apostle, only to recall him another day.

The other members of the group that had brought the collection found their way back to their homes in Galatia and about the Ægean. Paul's lieutenants stayed about him or came and went, carrying his messages and bringing him news of the work. Luke, Timothy and Tychicus we may assume were still near him or at his command. While not employed on Paul's errands, Luke was busy gaining the acquaintance with early Christian doings in Palestine that a generation later enabled him to write their story in the first part of what we know as The Acts of the Apostles. To the lively and educated young Greek doctor the memories that still lingered of Christian beginnings in Palestine twenty years before possessed extraordinary interest, and he naturally explored them as far as he possibly could.

His informants were numerous and notable. Philip and his gifted daughters lived right there in Cæsarea, and Luke may have again enjoyed their hospitality, as he had done on his arrival in Palestine. Of course, he could not actually share Paul's prison. In Jerusalem, such veterans as Peter and James he would delight to interview; as Hecataeus and Herodotus, coming like him from the cities on the Ægean, had interviewed priests and teachers as far as Egypt and Babylon a few centuries before. This historical curiosity was characteristic of intelligent Greeks, and Luke's stay in and about Cæsarea gave him opportunities to gratify it.

Willing as Felix was to listen to Paul from time to time, he showed no disposition to give him a real hearing and decide his case. Luke felt that Felix was putting the case off in the hope that Paul would offer him money to secure his release, and also for fear of angering the Jews if he let him go. Meantime, Felix was having troubles of his own. The rising power of the Sicarii in the cities and of Jewish guerilla bands in the countryside made the governor's life a burden. The disorder culminated in a Jewish demonstration in Cæsarea, where the Jews undertook to take possession of the city and dispossess the Greek and Syrian element which had always dominated the place. This absurd expression of nationalism finally came to open warfare, whereupon Felix intervened with his Roman soldiery and drove the Jews from the field with great slaughter. The Jews raised a great outcry against Felix over this, and he was recalled to Rome, where only the efforts of his brother Pallas, a favorite of Nero's, saved him. He lost his position, however, and was followed in the governorship by Porcius Festus.

Festus was a better man than Felix, but matters in Palestine had been steadily deteriorating for ten years and it was too late for him to save the situation. The Jews had succeeded in ousting his predecessor, and Festus naturally began with appeasement. Immediately upon his arrival in Cæsarea, he went up to Jerusalem to give the Jewish leaders a hearing, and one of their first demands was to have Paul brought to Jerusalem for trial. Festus told them Paul was being kept in custody in Cæsarea, and he was returning there himself. They could send their principal men there with him at once, and they could present their charges in Cæsarea, if there was anything wrong with Paul.

After a few days spent in Jerusalem, Festus returned to Cæsarea, and the next day he had Paul brought in and the Jews presented their charges. Paul declared that he had committed no offense against the Temple, the charge made against him two years before, or against the emperor. This last was a new accusation, like that made against him in Thessalonica, and seems to have been an effort to make Paul's preaching of Jesus as Messiah a denial of the authority of the emperor. Festus then asked him if he was willing to go up to Jerusalem for trial. Paul and his circle regarded the Jews' efforts to get him taken back to Jerusalem as a mere trap to bring him into the power of the organized Assassins there. He had twice escaped great personal danger there, and regarded a return to the Temple area as equivalent to a death sentence. But Festus, in his desire to conciliate the Jews, was evidently willing to expose Paul to this peril.

It was no fancied peril. These Jewish revolutionaries had killed their own high priest a few years before, and a few years later they were to kill the high priest Ananias, who was now managing the case against Paul. Their minds had been poisoned against Paul by reports from abroad, particularly by Jews from Ephesus, and the two years that had passed since the attack on Paul in Jerusalem had done nothing to mitigate their fury; on the contrary it was growing steadily hotter and more indiscriminate. The Romans, the Greeks, the Syrians, the high priests, the governor, Paul— it did not matter much who or what presented itself to the minds of the guerillas and Assassins; they were not long in developing a bitter and irreconcilable hatred that would stop at nothing. They were moving down the fatal path to open civil war, which in another decade would prove their own destruction. Paul's friends in Jerusalem were well aware of how matters were shaping there, and he was assured they were no better than when he had been rushed out of the city with a heavy Roman guard two years before.

Paul could not simply choose to be tried in Cæsarea; the governor was evidently ready to transfer the hearing of the case to Jerusalem, and the Jews were demanding it. He could not resist their combined demand. His only hope was to claim a Roman citizen's right, and appeal to the emperor's court in Rome. That would at least put him beyond the reach of the Jewish Assassins who were so relentlessly on his trail in Palestine. No doubt he had long since faced the possibility of the situation which had now arisen and resolved how to meet it, and he was ready with his answer.

"I am standing," he replied, "before the emperor's court, where I ought to be tried. I have done the Jews no wrong, as you can easily see. If I am guilty and have done anything that deserves death, I do not refuse to die; but if there is no truth in the charges that these men make against me, no one can give me up to them; I appeal to the emperor!"

This was a bold move which evidently took the governor somewhat by surprise, but after some conference with his judicial advisers he gave his decision.

"You have appealed to the emperor, and to the emperor you shall go!"

So Paul had his wish. He was at least extricated from the perils of Palestine, but would this inveterate Jewish hostility pursue him all the way to Rome? The Jewish authorities had their representatives, their lobby, there too, but in Rome he would at least be rid of mob violence and have the benefit of Roman justice, which had never yet wholly betrayed him. He went back to his prison quarters relieved in mind. He was to see Rome after all, meet some of the Christians there, and, he hoped, be set free for his mission to Spain.

The governor prepared to send Paul on to Rome for trial in company with a few other prisoners who must be sent there, and there was some little delay in forming the group and arranging for their sailing. Meantime, Festus was paid a state visit by King Agrippa II and his sister Bernice, who came over from Galilee to welcome him to his new post. They were Drusilla's brother and sister, being children of King Agrippa I, and Agrippa II was now king of the region about the Sea of Galilee, a position which he retained until about A.D. 100. The Emperor Claudius had given Agrippa the right to appoint the high priest in Jerusalem and, though he was only thirty, he had now been setting them up and deposing them for some years. He was consequently well versed in Jewish affairs, besides being a Jew himself, and through his great-grandmother Mariamne a descendant of the Maccabean line.

It was not unnatural, therefore, that Festus should think of consulting Agrippa about the charge he must forward with Paul to the emperor's court, which he did not know exactly how to formulate. He also thought that in view of Agrippa's position and antecedents he would be interested to see Paul and hear what he had to say.

"There is a man here," he told the king, "who was left in prison by Felix, and when I was at Jerusalem, the Jewish high priest and the elders presented their case against him and asked for his conviction. I told them it was not the Roman custom to give anybody up until the accused met his accusers face to face and had a chance to defend himself against their accusations. So they came back here with me, and the next day without losing any time I took my place on the bench and ordered the man brought in. But when his accusers got up, they did not charge him with any such crimes as I had expected. Their differences with him were about their own religion, and about a certain Jesus, who had died, but who Paul said was alive. I was at a loss as to how to investigate such matters, and I asked him if he would like to go to Jerusalem and be tried on these charges there. But Paul appealed to have his case reserved for his Majesty's decision, and I have ordered him kept in custody until I can send him to the emperor."

Agrippa indicated his interest in hearing what Paul had to say, and a hearing was accordingly arranged for the next day. Agrippa and Bernice came with their retinue, and the audience room of the palace was filled with officers and leading residents of Cæsarea. Festus ordered Paul brought in. Then the governor addressed the king and his guests, explaining the charges against Paul, the Jewish demand for Paul's death, Paul's appeal to the emperor's court, and his own perplexity as to what to charge him with.

"So I have brought him before you all," he concluded, "and especially before you, King Agrippa, in order to get from your examination of him something to put in writing. For it seems to me absurd to send a prisoner on, without stating the charges against him."

Agrippa said to Paul, "You are at liberty to speak in your own defense."

Paul willingly complied. He stretched out his hand with what must have been a characteristic gesture.

"I think myself fortunate, King Agrippa," he began, "that it is before you that I am to defend myself today against all the things the Jews charge me with, especially because you are so familiar with all the Jewish customs and questions. I beg you, therefore, to listen to me with patience. The way I lived from my youth up, spending my early life among my own nation and at Jerusalem, is well known to all Jews, for they have known from the first, if they are willing to give evidence, that I was a Pharisee, and my life was that of the strictest sect of our religion. Even now it is for my hope in the promise that God made to our forefathers that I stand here on trial—the promise in the hope of seeing which fulfilled our twelve tribes serve God zealously night and day. It is about this hope, your Majesty, that I am accused by some Jews.

"Why do you all think it incredible that God should raise the dead? I once thought it my duty vigorously to oppose the cause of Jesus of Nazareth. That was what I did at Jerusalem when on the authority of the high priests I put many of God's people in prison. When they were being put to death, I cast my vote against them, and many a time in all the synagogues I had them punished and tried to force them to say impious things. In my extreme rage against them I even pursued them to distant towns.

"I was once going to Damascus on this business, authorized and commissioned by the high priests, when on the road at noon, your Majesty, I saw a light from heaven brighter than the sun flash around me and my fellow travelers. We all fell to the ground, and I heard a voice say to me in Hebrew: 'Saul! Saul! Why do you persecute me? You cannot kick against the goad!' 'Who are you, sir?' I said. The Lord said: 'I am Jesus, whom you are persecuting. But get up, and stand on your feet, for I have appeared to you for the express purpose of appointing you to serve me and to testify to what you have seen and to the visions you will have of me. I will save you from your people and from the heathen, to whom I will send you to open their eyes and turn them from darkness to light, and from Satan's control to God, so that they may have their sins forgiven and have a place among those who are consecrated through faith in me.'

"Therefore, King Agrippa, I did not disobey that heavenly vision, but first to the people of Damascus and Jerusalem, and then all over Judea, and even to the heathen, I preached that they must repent and turn to God and live as men who have repented should. That is why the Jews seized me in the Temple and tried to kill me. To this day I have had God's help, and I stand here to testify to high and low alike, without adding a thing to what Moses and the prophets declared would happen, if the Christ was to suffer and by being the first to rise from the dead was to proclaim the light to our people and to the heathen."

By this time the Roman governor was far beyond his depth, and interrupted Paul.

"You are raving, Paul," he cried, "your great learning is driving you mad!"

"I am not raving, your excellency Festus," Paul answered, "I am telling the sober truth. The king knows about this, and I can speak to him with freedom. I do not believe that he missed any of this, for it did not happen in a corner! King Agrippa, do you believe the prophets? I know that you do!"

Agrippa turned this direct challenge with an evasive reply.

"You are in a hurry to persuade me and make a Christian of me," he retorted.

"In a hurry or not," said Paul, "I would to God that not only you but all who hear me today might be what I am—except for these chains!"

This dramatic appeal concluded the hearing, as Luke recorded it. The king rose and with the governor and the royal party left the audience room. Paul's companions heard afterwards that they all felt he had done nothing to be imprisoned for. Indeed, Agrippa said to Festus that if he had not appealed to the emperor he might have been released. But for that it was too late. He must be sent to Rome.

CHAPTER **XIX** ❧ THE GREAT VOYAGE

PAUL WAS a much traveled man. He had traveled the whole length of Asia Minor again and again, he had repeatedly crossed the Ægean, he had twice sailed the Mediterranean from Ephesus to Syria. But all these journeys were completely overshadowed by his voyage to Rome. His long-cherished dream of visiting the capital of the Roman world and helping to shape the religious faith of the Christian Church there was now to be fulfilled, but not as he had hoped. He was going as a prisoner, to be tried for his life. And yet he hoped to have some contact with the Christians of Rome. Two years had passed since he had written them his letter from Corinth, and it had been appreciated and answered. It had made him new friends in Rome, and he could count on their encouragement and support. This prospect gave a silver lining to the cloud of anxiety the prospect of his trial created. Not that he feared to die. He felt that death in the service of Christ was a noble experience, for it made one a partner in Christ's redemptive suffering.[1] But he did regret giving up his great work half done, and the consciousness of being laid aside, in a meaningless imprisonment, year after year, with the great missionary task to which he had set himself unfinished and lagging for want of him, made his situation doubly hard to bear. He was visited occasionally by Christians from abroad, and he undoubtedly maintained as active a correspondence with churches and individuals out in the Greek world as his prison conditions would permit.

The governor postponed despatching Paul to Rome longer than was wise, for the navigation of the Mediterranean ceased about November 11; indeed, navigation after the middle of September was considered dangerous, and going to sea in ships was not resumed until early in March. Perhaps Festus was waiting to assemble a group of prisoners, to be sent on to Rome under a single guard of soldiers, or perhaps he did not find a ship he was willing to send them by. It was early September before he had the prisoners, the guard and the sailing that he approved, and Paul and the other prisoners sailed.

Paul was attended by two of his friends from Macedonia, Aristarchus, of Thessalonica, and Luke, of Philippi. They must have accompanied him as his servants, or even his slaves, or they would not have been allowed to go with him. They were both members of the collection committee that had come east with him two years before and had evidently been in touch with him ever since, though they may have returned to Macedonia more than once in the interval. Certainly they formed points of contact for Paul with the churches in their respective cities. The characteristically Greek alertness of Luke to every situation gave interest for him to every stage and circumstance of the voyage.

The prisoners were in the charge of a Roman officer of the Imperial regiment named Julius. They sailed from Cæsarea on an Adramyttian ship, bound for the ports of Asia. Adramyttium was an Asian port, a little southeast of the city of Troas. The prisoners would have to transship when they reached the coast of Asia to a ship bound for Italy. Their first stop was Sidon, a remarkable run of more than eighty miles. There Julius, the Roman officer, allowed Paul to go ashore and see his Christian friends. Already there were coming to be Christian groups in every city on the coast. Putting to sea again, they sailed north, passing to the east of Cyprus and hugging the coast of Cilicia and Pamphylia, they reached the Lycian port of Myra, near the southwest corner of Asia Minor.

Myra was a port of some importance for Syrian and Alexandrian shipping, and the officer in charge of the prisoners found there an Alexandrian grain ship bound for Italy and transferred his party to it. The westerly winds that prevail in those waters and which had already retarded the Adramyttian ship held the Alexandrian vessel back as well, and she made slow progress for some days, at length making Cnidus, on the extreme southwest tip of Asia Minor, almost two hundred miles from Myra.

The Alexandrian ship on which the party was now traveling was one of the fleet of grain vessels plying between Alexandria and Italy, with the cargoes of wheat on which Rome depended for food. Some of them were large boats, capable of carrying four, five or six hundred people, in addition to their cargo. The winds which had already considerably delayed her progress continued so strong from the west and northwest that instead of sailing due west toward Italy she was forced to take to the southern side of Crete, and even there she made slow headway until she reached the harbor of Fair Havens, about midway of the length of the island, near the town of Lasea.

October was upon the travelers; the autumn fast of the Day of Atonement, probably October fifth, was past; and they were well into the "dangerous" period of navigation, between September 14 and November 11. Paul, who had seen a good deal of sea travel in his missionary journeys, tried to awaken the men in charge of the voyage to the danger of going farther at such a time of year and began to warn them of it. He seems to have had no difficulty in reaching them.

"Gentlemen," he said, "I see that this voyage is likely to end in disaster and heavy loss, not only to ship and cargo but to our own lives also."

The officer Julius, however, who was the man chiefly responsible, was more concerned with what the pilot and the captain had to say. Fair Havens did not appeal to them as a good harbor to winter in, and the general opinion favored putting to sea again and trying to reach another Cretan harbor, named Phoenix, which was said to face west-southwest and west-northwest and lay some sixty miles to the west. The long-desired south wind sprang up, and they set sail, keeping close to the coast of Crete. But the moment they turned the corner of Cape Matala, the most pronounced promontory on the Cretan coast, a violent northeaster swept down from the mountains and drove them out to sea. It was some hours before they were even able to get the ship's small boat, which had been towing behind, on board. The gale was so strong that they began to fear they might be carried clear across the Mediterranean and stranded on the Syrtis banks, west of Cyrene, so they lowered the sail and let the ship drift.

The next day the storm continued unabated, and to lighten the ship the men began to throw the cargo overboard. The third day they jettisoned all the tackle they could spare. For days the sky remained completely overcast; they could see neither sun nor stars, and so lost all sense of their position. Day after day the storm continued to rage. They no longer bothered to eat their meals. Their morale was gone. Hope died within them.

But not in the breast of Paul. It was now that he stood forth, with a call to courage and hope. The voice of God in his heart had given him fresh confidence. He would yet see Rome and face the emperor's court, and with him all his fellow travelers would win through. Some island would receive them and save them.

His appeals made little visible impression, but on the fourteenth night of the storm, as they drifted westward through the widest basin of the Mediterranean, which the ancients called the Adriatic, the sailors began to suspect that there was land ahead. They took soundings and found the water was rapidly growing shallow. Fearing rocks ahead, they cast four anchors from the stern and waited anxiously for daylight. The sailors lowered the ship's boat on the plea of running out anchors from the bow, but Paul suspected that they really meant to desert the ship and warned the officer. The soldiers cut the ropes that held the boat and let it drift away. The rest of the night Paul kept urging them all to eat something and recover their strength for the final emergency.

His protestations of hope revived their drooping spirits, and they followed his example and took some food.

PAUL

Paul was a good sailor or he could hardly have gone about among the storm-tossed company urging them to eat.

Daylight revealed a bay with a beach, and they cast off the anchors and hoisted the foresail in the hope of beaching the ship. But halfway in they struck a shoal or reef and the ship grounded and began to break up. The soldiers proposed to kill the prisoners to prevent their escape, but the officer prevented it. He had come to feel a good deal of respect for Paul and did not wish him sacrificed in this summary fashion. He ordered all who could swim to jump overboard and get to land, and the rest to float ashore on planks and pieces of wreckage. In the end, the whole ship's company of seventy-six, passengers, soldiers and crew, gained the land. Seven or eight years later Josephus, a young man of twenty-six, was shipwrecked in these same waters, on his way to Rome with some Jews being sent there for trial. After a night in the deep he was picked up with eighty fellow passengers by a ship of Cyrene which fortunately sighted them.

All the rest of their lives Paul's fellow travelers carried with them the memory of the courage and hopefulness he showed throughout this arduous experience, and at more than one crisis instilled into those about him. The general peril stripped away adventitious differences between prisoner and keeper, and revealed Paul as the real personality, the man of inward strength, who in the great emergency became the morale builder for them all.

This was Paul's fourth shipwreck.[2] On the island the castaways learned that it was Malta. In that terrible fortnight, they had sailed and drifted well over six hundred miles from

Lasea, in Crete, to their landfall on Malta, or an average of more than forty miles a day. In earlier times, people ship-wrecked on Greek islands in the Ægean had been sold as slaves, but at Malta the inhabitants treated the castaways with kindness, making a fire to warm and dry them, for it was cold and rainy. Paul bestirred himself to help in gather-ing fuel and was bitten by a snake hidden in a bundle of sticks he was putting on the fire. The natives thought he must be a wrongdoer, perhaps a murderer, who though he had managed to survive the sea, could not after all escape the demands of justice. But when he shook the crea-ture off into the fire and was none the worse, they changed their minds and concluded that he must be a god. The peo-ple were of old Phœnician stock and spoke a dialect derived from Punic.

The island lay fifty miles south of Sicily and belonged to that province. Paul was soon introduced, evidently by the officer Julius, to Publius, the head man of the island, who had estates in that part of it, and he welcomed the officer's party and entertained Paul and his companions for three days, when they were probably taken to lodgings in the town.

Malta is an island of some ninety square miles, seventeen and a half miles long by eight miles wide. The bay where the Alexandrian ship was wrecked was on the north side of the western extremity of it. The officer Julius naturally re-moved his charges to the chief settlement, the town of Malta, situated in the interior of the island, six or eight miles from the scene of the wreck. Here the officer and his party spent the winter. The winter climate is very mild, with a mean January temperature of about sixty degrees. At least the climate did not add to the troubles of the castaways.

While Paul's liberty was limited, he had some opportunity of contact with the townspeople, and they must have known some Greek, for Malta was a well-known stopping place for Mediterranean shipping. With Paul, Luke and Aristarchus detained there for three months, some missionary work was inevitable, and a Christian beginning must have been made. Sicily was frequently in plain sight, less than sixty miles north, with the stupendous mass of Etna visible in fair weather and, although the winter was no time for general navigation, some communication with Sicilian ports was not out of the question. Paul and Luke would be anxious to report their safety to their great circle of friends, especially in Rome and Philippi, and in all probability found means of doing so.

Those months shut up with Paul in the heart of Malta must have given Luke renewed opportunities even better than he could have had at Cæsarea or on their various voyages to hear Paul's recollections of his missionary travels and public addresses before they had met and become friends at Troas, and after they had parted. Luke's Greek curiosity would demand information about these matters in Paul's past, long before the idea of writing his history of Christian beginnings occurred to him.

As soon as navigation opened, according to Pliny on the seventh of February, but Vegetius says on the sixth of March, Julius embarked his party on another Alexandrian vessel, with the Dioscuri as figureheads, and sailed for Italy. The grateful Maltese provided the necessary supplies and gave them presents besides. The *Dioscuri* had wintered in the island, having probably reached it just ahead of the great storm, and been prevented by the lateness of the season from resuming its voyage after the storm. The splendid harbor of Malta would have been an ideal place for wintering.

The ship touched at Syracuse, about a hundred miles north, and spent three days there. Then they weighed anchor and called at Rhegium, their first Italian port, seventy-five miles farther. After a day there, a favorable south wind sprang up and two days' sail brought them to their destination, Puteoli, on the beautiful bay of Naples, the usual port of entry for ships from Egypt and the east, as Ostia was for those from Spain. Here Seneca, from his villa on the hillside, used to see the splendid spectacle of the arrival of the Alexandrian grain fleet from Egypt.

There were Christian brethren in Puteoli, and they urged Paul and his friends to stay with them for a week. This must have fitted the plans of the officer Julius, who was in charge of Paul, for it was arranged. Now word of Paul's arrival went up the Appian Way to Rome and the Christians there, and although he was coming as a prisoner on his way to trial the prospect of his arrival in Rome gave them great delight. Indeed, the very fact that he was a prisoner may have given his coming added interest, for he was a confessor and willing to be a martyr for their cause.

The Campanian Way left Puteoli by the Solfatara and led as directly north as the lay of the land permitted to Capua, famous old center of luxury, and now the most important place between Rome and Brundisium on the queen of Roman highways, the Appian Way. It was about the first of March, and travel was beginning to be brisk again. Capua was some twenty miles from Puteoli and was probably the travelers' first stop. Julius may have allowed Paul the use of a horse or mule, but such favors were hardly extended to his two attendants, one of whom may have been sent ahead by Paul to inform the Roman Christians of his approach. From Capua the Appian Way turned west to Sinuessa on the coast; it was there that Horace to his great delight was met by Vergil and two other friends of his on his way to Capua, almost a century before. A few miles farther the road reached Formiae, where Cicero had one of his favorite villas, and near which he had been put to death a hundred years before. Thence the road ran northwest to Fundi and then turned west to the sea again, to Anxur, eleven miles farther on, above Terracina. Thence it ran straight north through the Caecuban Hills and past the Pomptine Marches to the Market of Appius. From Feronia to the Market the journey could be broken by taking a boat on the canal that ran for almost twenty miles along the highway.

Meantime, Paul's friends had not forgotten him. When he left Cæsarea, or soon after, news of his movements had been sent to the church in Philippi, doubtless by Paul's devoted companion Luke, who was the charter member of the Philippian church, and his friends there had immediately raised a fund for the expenses of his stay in Rome and the costs of his defense there. As long as he was in Cæsarea, near his old friends in Antioch and the mother church at Jerusalem, they could safely leave such matters to the churches near at hand, but now that he was to appear in Rome, they felt that the responsibility was theirs. They also selected one of their number, a man named Epaphroditus, and despatched him to Rome with the money, to meet Paul on his arrival and do whatever was necessary for him.

It is most improbable that the Philippians deferred these steps until news reached them that Paul had actually arrived in Rome. That might be too late for any effective usefulness to him. Indeed, if they had waited for news of his arrival to reach them, and then told their messenger to make his way from Macedonia to Rome to offer his services, all might have been over before Epaphroditus made his appearance in Rome and began to look after Paul. Epaphroditus must have set out from Philippi soon after Paul left Cæsarea, fully expecting Paul to arrive in Rome within a few weeks. He would wait anxiously for his coming and only after weeks of apprehension learn that he had been shipwrecked and cast away on the island of Malta.

When upon Paul's landing in Puteoli it became possible for him to let the Romans know that he was at hand, Epaphroditus' long pent-up energies found expression. It must have been he who planned and organized the groups of Christians that went out from Rome, thirty and forty miles down the Appian Way, to Three Taverns and the Market of Appius to meet and welcome the long-awaited apostle. The Market of Appius was forty-three miles from Rome, a good two days' journey from the city, and it was a considerable undertaking for Roman Christians, few if any of whom belonged to the leisure class, to make such a journey. But between the letter to the Romans, which they had read or heard read in their church, and the activities of

Epaphroditus, who was acting as Paul's advance agent in Rome, this enthusiasm for the apostle's arrival becomes perfectly intelligible.

First at the Market of Appius well down the Appian Way, Paul was greeted and welcomed by a delegation of Roman Christians headed, we may well imagine, by Epaphroditus of Philippi, and then ten miles farther on at Three Taverns his Christian escort was swelled by another group eager to bid him welcome. Others were no doubt waiting to greet him on the outskirts of the city as he passed the towering tombs of the old patricians that lined the last miles of the ancient street.[3] Paul was hailed as a personage and made much of, and this reception made him, prisoner as he was, thank God and take fresh courage. So he came at last to Rome.

CHAPTER XX ❧ FROM A ROMAN PRISON

T HE LOYALTY and devotion of his old friends the Philippians combined with the eager anticipation of the Roman Christians, famous in the early church, as Hebrews afterwards said,[1] for their courageous support of their persecuted brethren, gave Paul's arrival in Rome something of the air of an ovation and even a triumph. Only a few years later Christians regarded martyrdom as a triumph, and their philosophy from the first was to welcome suffering endured for their great cause. Paul was turned over to the governor of the Foreign Camp, but with so good a report of his conduct and character that he was allowed more than usual liberty. He was permitted to live in lodgings outside the camp, where his friends could have free access to him, though a soldier was no doubt in constant attendance so that there would be no possibility of his escape.

Not that Paul lived in his own house in Rome; no one except the richest Romans did that. Rome was a city of great tenements, flat buildings, and apartment houses, in which the Romans had rooms or suites of rooms. Paul had such rooms in one of these great "insulae," or islands, as the Romans called them.

It was doubtless the liberality of the Philippians that made this favorable arrangement possible. Certainly Paul could no longer earn his living as he had done when he was at liberty, and the Philippians were sending him money to lighten the hardships of his imprisonment and if possible secure his acquittal. So they constituted themselves in effect a kind of ancient Red Cross or Prisoner's Aid for Paul's benefit. The feeling of friendlessness and abandonment to which prisoners are so liable was greatly relieved by their practical friendly concern.

One of Paul's first acts on reaching Rome and being assigned to these quarters, which Epaphroditus perhaps had in readiness for his arrival, was to write to the Philippians to thank them for all that they had done. But even before writing to them, he felt that he must meet and reach an understanding with the leading Jews of Rome. He wished to explain to them his real attitude, as in no sense an accuser of his own nation, but as holding that in Jesus Judaism had found its Messiah, and the fruition of its great religious hopes. They declared that they had had no instructions about him or against him from Jerusalem; the representatives of his Jerusalem accusers had not yet put in an appearance in the capital.

Paul was the more eager to write his letter of thanks to the Philippians because he had learned, probably from Epaphroditus, of the appearance of Judaizers in Philippi, although there was no synagogue there and this made their efforts to invade that city and interfere with the church there seem doubly uncalled for. These people with their pretensions of religious privilege because of their Jewish descent moved Paul to indignation, for he was just as pure-blooded an Israelite as they. But he has seen the worthlessness of all such pretensions compared with the religious experience of really knowing Christ, having faith in him, and experiencing union with him. This experience has revealed to him a spiritual goal toward which he presses forward, as they must do.

In the weary months of his imprisonment in Cæsarea he has learned one great lesson—to control his thoughts. It was bitter to have to waste his years in prison, with his great missionary task only half done, and left to lag in less competent hands, while he must sit idly by. But he has learned not to dwell on such things, but on happier, worthier, kindlier matters. That was the way to peace, and that is the way they must follow, if the peace of God is to guard their minds and thoughts.

How glad he is that they have again been moved to help him with a gift. Not that his happiness depends on the means at his disposal; he has learned the secret of contentment, whether he is rich or poor. He knows how to live humbly, and he knows how to enjoy plenty. His happiness does not depend on such things. But it is very kind of the Philippians to share his difficulties. He remembers how long ago, when he went on from them to Greece, no church but theirs went into business with him and became his partner. Even before that, when he first left Philippi for Thessalonica, they had more than once sent him money for his needs. And now they have renewed their interest in his financial requirements and sent him this gift by Epaphroditus. They have paid him in full, and more too! He is fully supplied, through what he has received from Epaphroditus. It is like fragrant incense, just such a sacrifice as God welcomes and approves. And God will gloriously requite them.

Again and again Paul bids them farewell. "Goodbye,

and the Lord be with you always. Again I say, good-bye." All God's people in Rome wish to be remembered to them, especially those who belong to the emperor's household.

Time went on. Paul's trial was strangely delayed and postponed. The papers in his case may have been lost in the shipwreck and others had to be secured from Festus at Cæsarea. Paul had other anxieties. Epaphroditus, the Philippians' representative, who had become very useful to him, had fallen seriously sick; in fact he came very near dying, and news of his condition had reached Philippi and greatly distressed the Philippians. Their agent, whom they had sent in the hope that he would be so useful to Paul, had now become an added care and anxiety to him.

But Epaphroditus did not die. He began to improve, and when at last he was well enough to travel Paul sent him back to Philippi. When he did so, he put into Epaphroditus' hand another letter to the Philippians, explaining his return. He did not wish the Philippians, when they saw Epaphroditus again on the streets of Philippi, to wonder at his return and ask him whether Paul had been acquitted, and if not, why he had left his place at Paul's side. Paul felt that Epaphroditus had done all he could do for him. In fact, he had risked his life for him.

Paul could never think of the Philippians without feelings of gratitude for their coöperation; from the very beginning of his acquaintance with them, it had never failed him. Even now, in prison, he feels that they are with him, sharing the great task of defending the right to preach the gospel. For Paul had come to see in his trial much more than just his personal fate; it was the right to preach the new faith that was at stake.

Whether Paul has already appeared before the emperor's court he does not definitely say, but he is certainly facing such an appearance; it is close at hand. When that ordeal comes, he will feel that the Philippians are at his side.

Paul is deeply concerned about the progress the gospel mission is making. His own arrest and imprisonment, so far from discouraging the brethren, have had the effect of rousing their courage and stimulating their activity. Some of them, it is true, were doing their work from jealousy and partisanship, while others did it out of good will. But all that mattered was that the gospel was being preached and Christ made known. For himself, his only concern was to play his part courageously and do Christ credit in whatever might befall him.

And that might be death. Paul was facing that possibility very definitely. He was perfectly ready for it; indeed, he longed to depart and be with Christ, which he thought was a far better fate than going on in this world. Yet he could see there was still a need for his work and that made it necessary for him to stay on. He hoped he would do so, and visit them again. For their part, they must never falter, but share in the struggle he was making. They must make Christ, in his humility and sacrifice, their model, and live like children of God in a crooked and perverted age. To Paul, Christians appeared like stars in the world's night, offering despairing men the message of life.

Timothy was with him, and he hoped soon to send him to Philippi to get news of them. But it is Epaphroditus who carries the letter, as he returns to Philippi after recovering from his illness.

Paul had a great reputation as a counselor and adviser upon questions that arose in the churches, and not only in the churches he had founded but in others which knew him only by reputation. Sometimes their representatives would make long journeys to lay their problems before him and get his views. This was a service that even in prison he could still render.

One of the problems brought to him in his Roman prison for solution had arisen in Colossæ, a hundred miles east of Ephesus, one of three cities close to one another in the valley of the Lycus River. The others were Hierapolis and Laodicea, and the gospel had come to them from Ephesus during Paul's three-year ministry there. Their minister was Epaphras, and he sought Paul in Rome to consult him. There had come into the church at Colossæ people of Greek education and background, who held the view that between man in his physical limitations and God in his goodness and greatness a vast gulf intervened. Yet between man and God there existed range after range of æons, virtues, or even beings, by communion with one after another of which man might by dint of reflection and self-discipline surmount this height and rise at last into the full experience of God, and complete fellowship with him.

When such people heard the gospel, they accepted it, recognizing in Christ one of these intermediaries communion with whom would help them on their way to God. Their ascetic practices—fasts, vigils and holy days—set them apart from ordinary believers, and they came to consider themselves a higher class of Christians, of superior spiritual attainment.

Three years of seclusion as a prisoner had developed and matured Paul's inward experience and his thought of Christ, and when he heard Epaphras' story of the Colossians' perplexity, it all welled up in a great tide. He had come to see in Jesus the embodiment of the divine Wisdom, (spoken of in The Wisdom of Solomon as with God in the beginning), which was the reflection of his nature, and through which he made the world. The very words of Wisdom, a book with which he had long been familiar, came back to his mind.[2] All the boasted intermediaries of the Colossian speculations were summed up in Christ, and all they had to give to the aspiring soul would be found in him.

As Paul's imprisonment lengthened, he came to feel that he was in some measure actually sharing in Christ's sufferings for the church, and making up as it were what was lacking in them.[3] Well aware that the Colossians were familiar with the mystery or initiation religions, he saw that there was also a Christian mystery—the reëmbodiment in believers of the spirit of Christ, which promised to glorify them. This promise was not for a select few but for all believers. In spreading the news of him, he warned everyone and taught everyone all the Christian wisdom, in order to bring everyone to Christian perfection. This was the great democratic ideal of the early Church as Paul envisioned it. Christians must not be misled by specious arguments, philosophic pretensions or ascetic practices. They must fix their thoughts on the things that are above and treat their old passions as dead and gone. They have put on a new nature, and all the old distinctions of race, nation and position, slave or free, had passed away; Christ is everything and in them all.

In hours of reflection, in the enforced idleness of Paul's long months in prison, a vision of truly Christlike behavior had formed itself in Paul's mind—of tenderness of heart, kindness, humility, gentleness, forbearance. Christians must learn to forgive, as the Lord had forgiven them. Love, peace, thankfulness—these must be the watchwords of the followers of Christ. All this Paul compressed into a letter and sent by the hand of Tychicus to the church at Colossæ.

Paul was keenly sensible of his great need of clearness and force in making his defense at his trial, now close at hand. His friends and lieutenants were gathering around him— Timothy, Tychicus and Aristarchus, who had all been members of the collection committee, Barnabas' cousin Mark, Jesus Justus, Luke and Demas, as well as Epaphras of Colossæ, and a young man named Onesimus. Their greetings go with his own to the brethren in the churches on the Lycus River.

When Tychicus set off from Rome on his long journey down the Appian Way to Brundisium, across to Corinth, and on across the Ægean to Ephesus and then overland to Colossæ and Laodicea, he did not go alone. There went with him this young man Onesimus, one of the least and yet one of the most significant of Paul's friends.

For he was a slave who had run away from his master Philemon, in Laodicea, robbing him of enough to make good his escape and continue it to distant lands. Somehow he had found his way to Rome and there come in touch with Paul and become part of his circle. Perhaps he had confided his story to Paul, or perhaps the coming of Epaphras from Colossæ had led to his identification. Epaphras had been concerned with the churches in Hierapolis and Laodicea as well as with the one in Colossæ, and doubtless knew Philemon, the master from whom Onesimus had run away.

Paul had become greatly attached to the youth and took a deep interest in his future. But he knew that there could be no secure life in the Roman world for Onesimus as a runaway slave. He must go back to his master and make a fresh start. This he persuaded Onesimus to undertake to do.

In doing this Paul took a tremendous risk. Some otherwise reasonable and humane masters believed in stern measures where runaway slaves were concerned. The slave population of the empire was larger than the free population, and a slave uprising was always a fearful possibility. The enslavement of whole cities like Corinth, years before, had made many capable and intelligent people slaves, so that there was plenty of competent leadership for such an enterprise. Many slaves were more educated and gifted than their owners. There was no telling what Philemon would think it his duty to do to Onesimus in the way of making an example of him; he might even treat him with such cruelty as to cause his death. Slaves were examined under torture when their testimony was needed. Paul was risking the life of Onesimus when he sent him back to Philemon.

Naturally Paul did all that he could to protect the young man. He wrote a letter to Philemon, telling him of his great affection for Onesimus, and asking him to receive him kindly, not as a slave but as a brother Christian. Anything Onesimus has stolen from Philemon, Paul undertakes to make good. He goes farther than this. He says he would have liked to keep Onesimus with him, to wait on him while he is in prison. Sending him back to Philemon, he says, is like sending his very heart. He would not, of course, keep him in Rome without Philemon's consent, but he makes it clear that what he really wants is not just to have Onesimus pardoned and taken back into Philemon's household but to have him returned to Paul in Rome, to continue to wait on him, as Paul puts it, in Philemon's place. Paul says quite frankly that he could order Philemon to do what ought to be done, but he prefers to appeal to him in the name of love, simply as what he is—Paul, no less an envoy of Christ Jesus, though now a prisoner for him. For his present position as a prisoner for his faith in the eyes of all true believers rather enhanced his authority. He might be on his way to martyrdom!

Philemon might still think his duty to the empire and to the slaveholding class, to which he belonged, justified him in taking severe measures with the runaway, and making his case a warning to any other restless spirits among the slaves of Laodicea. Is there anything Paul can possibly do to protect Onesimus? Yes, he can address his letter not simply to Philemon but to Archippus and Apphia, probably Philemon's wife, and the church that meets in Philemon's house. This will necessitate the settlement of Onesimus' case virtually in the presence of the whole Christian group to which Philemon belongs. Archippus was probably the leader of it, its minister, as we would say. The social pressure of the whole little group will be brought into play on Onesimus' behalf, should it be needed.[4]

Nor is this all. From Laodicea, Tychicus would go on eastward eleven miles to Colossæ to deliver Paul's letter to the church there. At the end of it the Colossians would read these instructions: "When this letter has been read to you, have it read to the church at Laodicea also, and see that you read the letter that is coming from there. And tell Archippus, 'See that you perform the Christian service you have been assigned.'" Archippus is evidently at Laodicea, which has just been mentioned, and has some connection with the letter that is coming from there. Had he been a Colossian, it would not have been necessary to instruct the Colossians to "tell" him Paul's message; he would have been present in their meeting, and would have been addressed directly: "And you, Archippus, see that you perform the Christian service you have been assigned." He is evidently elsewhere, and presumably at Laodicea. His Christian service evidently is to see that Philemon treats Onesimus at least humanely and, if possible, accedes fully to Paul's wishes.

But if the Colossian and Laodicean churches are to exchange letters, then the case of Onesimus is to have full publicity among the Christians of both places, and all that Christian opinion can do to influence Philemon's action will be done. If Philemon complies with Paul's wishes, the Christians of the whole countryside will approve and applaud his action. If he meditates harsher measures, the opinion of his fellow Christians will be effectively arrayed on the slave's side, and, such is the force of social pressure, will save him. So much even from his distant prison in Rome, Paul could and did do in this extraordinary situation.

Did he succeed? When Philemon at Laodicea heard the

letter from Colossæ read, he heard Paul say, "You who are masters must treat your slaves justly and fairly, and remember that you have a Master too, in heaven." Both the letters bearing on the Onesimus incident, for Colossians speaks of Onesimus very particularly and warmly, were preserved, and that suggests that they had been obeyed. There is some reason to suppose that the Onesimus who was bishop of Ephesus fifty years later may be identical with the slave boy for whom Paul interceded so eloquently in the little letter to Philemon. That is plainly suggested by Ignatius' letter to the Ephesians, about A.D. 110; and while it is by no means certain, no serious objection can be raised against it.

The correspondence with Philippi, the questions brought to Paul for solution from Colossæ, the problem of Onesimus —these are but samples of the sort of thing that occupied Paul's enforced idleness at Rome. He had also the exigencies of his trial to prepare for and meet. How did it come out and what was his fate?

Over these questions history has drawn a veil, and the modern biographer of Paul can do little better. When The Acts was written about A.D. 90, Paul was dead, but the great cause to which he had given the "last full measure of devotion"—the Greek mission—had gone on to great conquests and seemed to Paul's old friend and physician Luke to demand a historian. When the Roman church, about 95, wrote to the church of Corinth the letter we know as I Clement, Paul and Peter stood together in Christian memory at Rome as their great martyrs. Dionysius of Corinth, about 170, refers to Paul's martyrdom in Rome. Tertullian of Carthage, about 198–200, declared that Paul was beheaded in Rome. Gaius of Rome, early in the third century, refers to Paul as having suffered martyrdom on the Ostian Way. A little later Origen wrote that Paul suffered martyrdom in Rome under Nero, that is, 54–68. Eusebius, in 326, makes a similar statement. On the whole, the testimony of antiquity on the subject is clear and unanimous.

It is evident that Paul's trial ended in his conviction, probably as a disturber of the peace of the empire and a center of disorder, possibly also as proclaiming another king than the emperor. As a Roman citizen he would be sentenced to die by the sword.[5] He had long since adjusted himself to such a fate. It was the Christian's privilege not only to trust in Christ but also to suffer for him. As a prisoner he had felt that he was in his own measure making up what was lacking in Christ's sufferings. As far as he was concerned, he longed to depart and be with Christ. Four or five years before he had written to the Romans his great valedictory: "Who can separate us from Christ's love? Can trouble or misfortune or persecution or hunger or destitution or danger or the sword? . . . But in all these things we are more than victorious through him who loved us. For I am convinced that neither death nor life . . . will be able to separate us from the love God has shown in Christ Jesus our Lord!"

CHAPTER XXI ❧ THE RETURN OF PAUL

P AUL WAS a man of extraordinary vigor and originality, and his emancipation from the trammels of Judaism released his powers and gave them scope. His tireless journeyings about the eastern empire, his missionary preaching often in the face of bitter opposition and much personal violence, his pioneering spirit, which led him to preach Christ in regions where he had not been proclaimed before, created before the minds of his Christian contemporaries the classic figure of the Christian missionary. More than any other he had seen and served the needs of the Greek mission, and he stood out as par excellence the apostle to the Gentiles. So for a generation he lived in Christian memory as a great doer, a man of action, who had carried the gospel to new provinces—Cyprus, Galatia, Macedonia, Greece, Asia—eloquent in his preaching, heroic in facing danger, strong in his faith, who had finally sealed his teaching with his blood, as the first of the Roman martyrs.

The great forces he had done so much to release swept on into increasing power. That Greek world to which he had introduced Christianity was preëminently a reading world, and for it Gospels began to be written—Mark, at Rome, and Matthew, probably at Antioch. Christians were taking up the literary techniques of the time to give the new generation of believers the books it demanded about Jesus and the beginnings of its faith, now half a century and more in the past. Luke, the Third Gospel, appeared at Ephesus, but not as a single book, like the others, but as volume one of a two-volume survey of Christian beginnings down to the establishment of the Greek mission, by A.D. 90 in full swing. Christianity had developed a reading public, and Christians were doing their utmost to meet its new demands, and with great success.

As for Paul's letters, they had done what he wrote them to do, but they were so closely interwoven with the church problems and personalities of their time that as these faded into the past the letters faded with them. They were not written for publication, and they fell into the soil of the church and were forgotten. A few of the longer ones were preserved in the churches to which they had been addressed, and were occasionally read in them, perhaps on the anniversary of Paul's martyrdom. But when Christians began to write books, ten years and more after the death of Paul, Christian writers showed no acquaintance with Paul's letters. Mark, being written in Rome, reflects slight touches of Romans, but of no others, while Matthew, written probably in Antioch, and Luke and Acts, written probably in Ephesus, disclose no knowledge of any letters written by Paul, though the letters would have given Luke important information as to the purpose back of some of Paul's movements. It is plain that the letters as a whole were quite unknown in these greatest centers of first-century Christianity, even to the men who were laying the foundations of Christian literature, in writing the earliest Gospels.

People still remembered Paul, in all his zeal and power,

but it is nothing strange that he did not particularly impress his generation as a writer of letters. The Corinthians knew he had written them letters, mostly unwelcome ones, but they knew nothing of his letters to other churches. And for all his churches, his personal work, in preaching, journeying, facing mobs and riots, and the like, were the things for which they most admired and loved him. For them and for him, his letter-writing was but a minor incident of his tumultuous career. It was only long after the living man had passed from the scene that his written letters began to rise into significance.

Thirty years after Paul's death, the publication of Luke's two-volume work, with its commanding picture of Paul, shown in such a series of dramatic scenes, the martyrdom of Stephen, Paul's conversion, his escape from Damascus, his facing the mobs, his appearances before governors and kings, his shipwreck—all this brought the figure of Paul to life for the new Christian generation and revived interest in him as such biographical narratives still do for their subjects.

What a man he had been! If only he had lived in those days when Christians were awakening to the use of books in the spread of the gospel! If he could be called back to the missionary task in this new age of books, what books he could write! It would be like rousing a giant from his sleep. Why, some of his letters were almost books. And somewhere in the churches he had written to, the idea arose of publishing any letters of his that they still possessed.

The only thing remotely resembling a collection of his letters was the combination of the letters to the Colossians and the Laodiceans, which he had himself unconsciously caused, when he instructed the Colossians to exchange letters with Laodicea. Both churches would thus, naturally, become possessed of Colossians and Philemon. It was probably some Christian of Asia who took up the idea, perhaps a former Colossian or Laodicean, perhaps even Onesimus himself, to whom the tiny letter to Philemon had brought freedom and opportunity; certainly to no one else could it have meant so much. It was probably at Ephesus that the plan was developed and carried out, for when it was, the short letter of introduction that Paul gave to Phoebe to take with her to Ephesus was included, at the end of Romans.

The Acts, with its revelation of Paul's journeys and missions, to Galatia, Macedonia, Greece and Asia, would give the man who wanted to collect Paul's letters the names of the churches he had founded, some of which might still possess letters from his hand. The Acts recorded the names of many cities where he had lived and preached and presumably established churches: Antioch, Iconium, Lystra, Derbe—the churches of Galatia; Philippi, Thessalonica, Berea, Athens, Corinth, Ephesus and finally Rome. To write to these, or even if necessary to visit them in search of letters from Paul that might survive in their church chests, along with the manuscripts of the Greek Old Testament from which they read in church, would be no very difficult task, especially after The Acts had so stimulated interest in Paul, and the churches everywhere were so aroused to the values of a Christian literature. What a magnificent thing it would be if some letters of Paul had survived and could be assembled! It would be like bringing him back once more upon the missionary scene. As many a modern is stirred by some notice of a figure of a past generation to search for forgotten letters of his, so these alert first-century Christians, who were so energetically adopting and developing the familiar pagan techniques of publication, sought out, collected, published and put into circulation the long-neglected letters of Paul.[1]

Certainly the nine letters we possess from the hand of Paul did not collect themselves. Still less did they automatically slip into their places in a Pauline collection as soon as they were written and sent. They were bona fide letters, sent to the persons for whom they were meant, without any preservation of duplicate copies at their source by the author or his amanuensis, such as the younger Pliny practiced in his letter book. When in later years Pliny published his "collected" letters, he had even improved the style of some of them over the form in which he had first sent them to the persons to whom they were addressed. No such artificiality attached to the original Pauline collection.

The collector of Paul's letters was richly rewarded. In the first place, he was enabled to read all Paul's extant letters, being obviously the first man to do so. The effect upon him was tremendous. A new vision of the depth and sweep of Christian experience flashed upon his spirit. It was probably under its influence that he wrote the splendid introductory letter, summing up Paulinism, with which he prefaced the published collection, and which we know as Ephesians. The oldest manuscripts show that it was addressed to no individual church but to Christians everywhere, and in it every one of the nine letters he had discovered is reflected.

The effect of this publication of Paul's letters was in

every way remarkable. Up to that time no Christian writer had shown any acquaintance with them; after it every Christian writer knew them and felt their influence.[2] Nor was this all. The appearance of the collected letters focused Christian attention not only upon what Paul had to say in them but upon the published letter as an ideal form of Christian instruction, and it immediately became and for some time remained the favorite form of Christian literary expression. The Revelation of John was so affected by it and by the whole Pauline collection that, although it is an apocalypse, a wholly different kind of literature, it is introduced by a collection of letters to Christian churches, seven in number, prefaced by a general letter to all seven. Nor were these letters in the Revelation actually sent to the individual churches they address and then laboriously gathered from them to form the collection; not at all. They were written as a collection, and all sent to all the churches in the list. The artificial character of this is obvious. It is a literary device, suggested by the Pauline collection of letters to Christian churches, seven in number, and prefaced by a general letter to all seven. The writer of the Revelation had seen the newly published collection of Paul's letters and was so impressed by it that he patterned the portal of his apocalypse upon it.

As the Revelation of John was written late in the reign of Domitian, who was assassinated in A.D. 96, the collection and publication of Paul's letters must have been accomplished between A.D. 90 (about which time Luke wrote his two volumes) and 95. This is confirmed by the influence of the Pauline collection on the Epistle to the Hebrews, written to the Roman church during the same period of stress and so strongly influenced by Paul's letters that the ancients actually ascribed it to Paul. Paul's letters are first definitely quoted in I Clement, a letter written by the Roman church to the Corinthians, about 95, which refers to I Corinthians as written to the Corinthians by Paul, and shows the influence of most of the other letters.

The spur Hebrews had applied to the Roman church, in saying it ought by this time to be teaching the other churches,[3] led the Roman Christians to look about for other evils in the churches which they might correct, and they wrote I Peter, setting forth a nobler, gentler attitude to persecution than the Revelation had advocated. The use of Paul's letters is very marked; six of them are clearly reflected in the letter.

Twenty years later the writer of the Gospel of John saw fit to use the letter as well as the Gospel as a medium for his message, and in his time Ignatius of Antioch, on his way through Asia to martyrdom in Rome, was led to write letters to six churches about the Ægean and one to the bishop of Smyrna. This bishop, Polycarp, soon after wrote a letter to the church at Philippi. The letters of James and Jude, the letter of Barnabas, the Epistle of the Apostles, the letters to Timothy and Titus, the letter known as the Martyrdom of Polycarp, and the Second Letter of Peter show how popular the letter form of Christian instruction became after the publication of Paul's letters and how long this popularity continued. It was not the original writing and sending of Paul's letters that precipitated this letter-writing movement in the church; it was the collecting and publishing of them that so impressed Christian teachers with the possibility of the published letter as a means of Christian instruction.

It will be seen that the publication of Paul's collected letters also led to the writing and publishing not only of individual letters but of whole letter collections by subsequent Christian leaders. There is the group of letters at the beginning of the Revelation, which so closely reflects the Pauline collection in scope (letters to seven churches) and organization (preceded by a general letter to all seven). There are the letters of John, a general letter to the Christians of Asia, a letter to a church, and a letter to a member of that church. There are the letters of Ignatius, mostly to churches, which seem to have had no individual circulation at all but were immediately (even before news of Ignatius' death at Rome had had time to reach Polycarp at Smyrna) put in circulation by Polycarp from Smyrna. There were the pastoral letters, to Timothy and Titus, written soon after A.D. 150, and circulated together as a supplement to the Pauline collection. A little later there was a group of letters bearing the name of other apostles, Peter, John and Jude, which sought to do for the apostles what had long before been so successfully done for Paul—assemble and publish their letters.

But above and beyond all this was the influence Paul's letters, as soon as collected and published, began to exert upon the thought and life of the church. In his splendid teachings of faith, love, tolerance, the true fruits of the Spirit, the right kind of life, his voice was heard again and gave a great reinforcement to the moral and spiritual life of the church, while his great idea of Christ as the incarnation of God's creative wisdom entered vitally into the Gospel of John and greatly affected Christian theology. Jesus was not the denial of the divine wisdom and intelligence; he was the embodiment of them. So John became the Pauline Gospel. The opening lines of it show the influence of Col. 1:15–19, which guided the Evangelist to Wisdom 9:1, 2, 9, so clearly reflected in his prologue. Paul's great doctrine of the love of God, Rom. 5:1–11, is nobly summarized in the most loved and quoted verse in John, 3:16. And all this Pauline teaching culminates in the great affirmation in the First Epistle: "God is love!" So for theology and ethics Paul greatly influenced the Evangelist John.

When the Gospel of John was combined, about A.D. 115, with those of Matthew, Mark and Luke, to form the fourfold Gospel, the influence of Paul upon Gospel thought was perpetuated and enhanced. Thirty years later the four Gospels were being read in church as Christian Scripture, side by side with the Old Testament. A few years more, and Paul's collected letters too were being read in church, as part of the Christian "Bible"—the Books, par excellence. From that time on, Paul has spoken with renewed authority, and at intervals great Christian leaders, like Augustine and Luther, have found prodigious stimulus in him. More and more his great social and religious ideas—faith, freedom, tolerance, democracy, solidarity, kindness, hope, love, good will, the new life, the indwelling Spirit, the appropriation of "the mind of Christ," communion with God—have repeatedly reinforced the Christian Church. John foresaw that the Spirit would eventually guide the believer into all truth.

It was not the Paul pictured by Luke who accomplished all this and still so largely holds the church upon her course; it was the Paul of the letters, who in them had come back as a living force to carry forward the work on which he had been so actively engaged. In them Paul lived and spoke again and renewed his great campaign, only begun in the twenty years of his mission work, and in them he is still at work, bold, incisive, regardless of rhetoric except the vital native kind his thought itself developed, trenchant, penetrating, profound.

Certainly Paul has dominated Christian theology ever since the first century, and he is still revealing new moral values in the mid-twentieth. It was he who saw in the struggling Jewish sect of the Nazarenes the great world religion Jesus came to found, and proclaimed and established it. It was his letters, exhumed and published thirty years after his death, that brought the Christian movement a spiritual, moral and intellectual reinforcement of immense value. It was as if Paul himself had come back to lead a fresh attack upon the principalities and the powers of ancient paganism, and his letters have remained through the centuries and still are among the most potent, dynamic and enduring literary forces in the world.

CHRONOLOGY

A.D.

10–15 Birth

34   Conversion

36   Return to Jerusalem

36–46 In Cilicia, principally Tarsus

46–47 In Antioch

47–48 First Missionary Journey

47   Visits Cyprus

48   Council in Jerusalem

49–52 Second Missionary Journey

50–51 In Corinth

50   Writes I, II Thessalonians

52   Writes Galatians

52–56 Third Missionary Journey

52–55 In Ephesus

53–55 Writes I, II Corinthians

56   Winter in Corinth

56   Writes Romans

56   Arrest in Jerusalem

56–58 In Cæsarea

59–61 In Rome

59–61 Writes Philippians, Colossians, Philemon

61   Martyrdom

92–94 His letters first collected and published

NOTES

Chapter I

[1] Some scholars have maintained that in the synagogues of the Dispersion the Law and the Prophets were not read in Hebrew, a dead language, of course, but in the familiar Greek of the Septuagint version. They have gone on to the view that Paul knew little if any Hebrew and point to the fact that he usually quotes the Old Testament in the Septuagint version, not in his own translation of the Hebrew. This can hardly be considered a very serious argument, however, since scores and perhaps hundreds of ministers well trained in Hebrew in seminaries constantly quote the Old Testament in published translations instead of resorting to the Hebrew for its meaning. In fact, in their public use of the Old Testament, they resort to the Hebrew on the whole more rarely than Paul did in his use of it in his letters. In this course Paul, like the modern minister, had in mind in part his public, which of course recognized only the standard version. That Paul should have gone to Jerusalem to study to be a rabbi without knowing Hebrew is most improbable, but if he did so, on arriving there he must have made great haste to repair that deficiency. With his familiarity with Aramaic, this would not be difficult. Of his devotion to the "tradition" he says himself that he surpassed many of his own age in his devotion to Judaism, he was so

fanatically devoted to what his forefathers had handed down. (Gal. 1:14.) That he studied under Gamaliel, as Acts declares, is not negatived by the divergence of the type of Judaism he attacks in Galatians and Romans from what is known of Gamaliel's teachings; Gamaliel was not his sole source of information on Pharisaism, not to mention Sadduceeism, and few modern scholars perpetuate their great teachers' positions unaltered. The view that the Jewish synagogues out in the western provinces of the empire did not have the Scripture read in Hebrew, but only in Greek, would leave the traditional Jewish practice in that matter unexplained, and leave even the preservation of the Hebrew Bible through the Middle Ages a problem.

Chapter II

[1] Lev. 24:16; Deut. 13:10.

[2] While the lexicons say "young man," *neanias*, may be twenty-four to forty years old (citing Phrynichus and Diogenes Laertius, II-III centuries), Luke's usage restricts this considerably. He uses it not only of Paul in ch. 7 but in ch. 20 of Eutychus who fell asleep during Paul's sermon and fell out of the window and of Paul's nephew who got wind of the plot against Paul and reported it, ch. 23. Neither of these occurrences suggests maturity; the nephew is called *neaniskos* in vs. 18 in some texts; the case of Eutychus precludes it, for he is spoken of later as *ho pais*, "The lad," Acts 20:9; 23:17, 22. With Luke the word evidently means a young man between eighteen and twenty-five.

Early uses of *neanias* are on the younger side; Odyssey 10:278: "a young man, with the first down on his lip, the time when youth is most gracious." So is the latest use I have noted, in Oxyrhynchus Papyri, 471:114 (II century A.D.), where (if the reconstruction is correct) it is used of boys around seventeen! The use of *presbutes* of Paul in Philemon has no bearing on the question as it means "envoy" or "ambassador," not "aged," or "old man in that place."

The unfavorable description of Paul's physique in the second-century *Acts of Paul* as "a man little of stature," etc., is probably drawn from his name Paulus—Parvulus, Parvus, "Small," "Little"—combined with a misunderstanding of II Cor. 10:10, which simply meant that the Corinthians were momentarily out of patience with Paul. Paulus had long been a well-known Latin surname, e.g. Lucius Æmilius Paulus, Roman general at Cannae, 216 B.C., and his son of the same name, who defeated Perseus of Macedon at Pydna, 168 B.C.

³ Deut. 17:7.
⁴ See also Gal. 1:13.
⁵ I Cor. 9:5.

Chapter III

¹ Rom. 2:19.
² II Cor. 11:24.
³ Deut. 25:1-4.
⁴ In The Acts Luke speaks as if Saul now returned at once to Jerusalem, where the brethren would at first have nothing to do with him, until Barnabas talked with him and became convinced of the sincerity of his Christian profession and introduced him to the apostles. He then began to preach and debate with the Greek-speaking Jews, until the Jews

once more plotted to kill him and the brethren accordingly took him down to Cæsarea and sent him home to Tarsus. They evidently regarded him as too much of a storm center to serve the cause just then in Jerusalem.

But long before The Acts was written, Paul in writing to the Galatians puts the matter very differently. It was not until three years after his journey to Damascus that he found his way to Jerusalem, and then he met none of the leaders of the brotherhood except Peter, and James the brother of Jesus. Nor did he on that visit engage in active work among the brethren; on the contrary, they did not know him, but only heard that their former persecutor had now joined their ranks. Paul says this so explicitly and solemnly that it must be the truth about his first visit as a Christian to Jerusalem, Gal. 1:18–23.

Chapter IV

[1] Luke says the Greek-speaking Jews in Jerusalem were so incensed at Paul that they tried to kill him and that the brethren "when they found it out, took him down to Cæsarea and sent him away to Tarsus." (Acts 9:29, 30.)

[2] Acts 11:26; 26:28; I Peter 4:16.

[3] While The Acts describes Barnabas and Saul as carrying the Antioch collection to Jerusalem, 11:30; 12:25, this is contrary to Paul's own account of his visits to Jerusalem in Gal. 1:18 to 2:1, which leave no room for such a visit. The narrative of Acts says nothing of anything done by Paul on this relief visit; he appears simply as the companion of Barnabas. Luke probably assumed that as he had helped to raise the money he would go with Barnabas to deliver it.

But had he done so, Paul could not have omitted it from his painstaking account of all his contacts with Jerusalem, in Gal. 1, 2.

⁴ There is no real reason to doubt Papias' statement to that effect (ca. A.D. 140) in one of the surviving fragments of his lost "Interpretations of the Sayings of the Lord." "Mark," he wrote, "having become the interpreter of Peter, wrote down accurately everything that he remembered, without, however, recording in order what was either said or done by Christ. For neither did he hear the Lord speak, nor did he follow him, but afterwards, as I said, attended Peter, who adapted his instructions to the needs of his hearers, but had no design of giving a connected account of the Lord's oracles." That is to say, Peter did not set out to compose a gospel, but Mark, who served as his interpreter and would translate his Aramaic sermons to his Greek-speaking congregations at Rome, after Peter's death gathered from his memories of them the parts that preserved Peter's recollections of Jesus.

Chapter V

¹ See D. G. Hogarth, *Devia Cypria*, pp. 114, 115. The inscription is dated in the thirteenth year (of Claudius), A.D. 52–53, and tells of a certain Apollonius who had revised the list of members of the local senate "in the time of Paulus the governor," as if Paulus had been governor no long time before.—A Sergius, possibly the same man, is mentioned by the elder Pliny, *Natural History*, II, 113, and a Sergius Paulus occurs at the beginning of Bk. XVIII, in his lists of authors or authorities used by him, but here some texts read

"Sergius Plautus," so that we cannot build much if anything upon the name. A Sergius Paulus who may be the Cyprus governor is mentioned in a Latin inscription, C.I.L. vol. vi, no. 31545.

Chapter VI

[1] A hundred years after Paul's visit to Iconium, Christian fancy clothed his work there with romance in the story of Thecla, a beautiful young Greek girl of high position, who heard him preach, and was converted, refusing marriage and escaping martyrdom to become a Christian teacher and preacher in her country. This story, which has for centuries been widely read in the original Greek or in half a dozen versions, is now known to have been just the most popular chapter in a religious novel, the *Acts of Paul*, written about A.D. 160–170, long lost but now for the most part recovered in a Coptic version (1896) and, for the closing scenes, in the Greek original (1936).

As for Thecla, as great a historian as Harnack has declared that it was "unlikely that the romancer simply invented this figure. There must have really been a girl converted by a Paul at Iconium, whose name was Thecla, and who took an active part in the Christian mission." Certainly to this day the twin cones of St. Philip and St. Thecla attract the traveler's eye as he looks westward from the site of Iconium. See Harnack, *Mission and Expansion of Christianity in the First Three Centuries*, II, p. 73.

Iconium played a leading part in the life of Asia Minor from the twelfth to the fourteenth centuries, when it was the capital of the Seljuk Turkish empire, and the seat of its sultan.

[2] F. M. Derwacter, *Preparing the Way for Paul*, 1930.

Chapter VII

[1] *Merchant of Venice*, i, 3, 36–38.
[2] Lev., chs. 17; 18.
[3] Hos. 6:6.
[4] Mic. 6:8.

Chapter VIII

[1] Ecclus. 38:12.
[2] It is much more probable that the use of the first person plural seventy-seven times in the narrative of Acts means that the writer of the book is present on these occasions than that in them he is using a "we" document or diary he had found, and forgetting that it is not his own diary mistakenly quotes it seventy-seven times as if it were. See Ch. XVI, note 1.
[3] *History*, i, 4.
[4] Eccles. 7:28; Ecclus. 42:9, 10; Prov., ch. 31.
[5] I Cor. 1:11; 16:19; Rom. 16:1, 3; Acts 18:2, 18, 26.

Chapter IX

[1] Pausanias in his *Description of Greece* (ca. A.D. 175) speaks of seeing at Phalerum, the old port of Athens, an altar to an unknown God (J. G. Frazer, *Pausanias and Other Greek Sketches*, p. 203). Frazer goes on, "In a dialog attributed to Lucian (125–200) a certain Critias . . . swears by the Unknown God of Athens." But this dialog is

now assigned to a much later date. See Pausanias, *Description of Greece*, i.1.4, v.14:8; Deissmann, *St. Paul*, Appendix II.

[2] A similar line occurs in an earlier Greek poet, Cleanthes, in his *Hymn to Zeus*, 4 (ca. 300 B.C.).

Chapter X

[1] Byron, *The Curse of Minerva*.

[2] Suetonius says that Claudius expelled the Jews from Rome, *Claudius* 25, adding the mysterious explanation "*impulsore Chresto*": "*Iudaeos impulsore Chresto adsidue tumultuantes Roma expulit.*" Orosius (fifth century), vii, 6, 15, also states it, on the authority of a certain Josephus (apparently not the famous Jewish historian) and assigns it to the ninth year of the reign of Claudius, i.e., probably A.D. 49. This accords well with the presence of Aquila and Prisca in Corinth in 50, having as Luke says "recently come from Italy," Acts 18:2.

[3] I Thess. 4:9–12.

[4] II Thess. 2:3–10.

[5] 1:14.

[6] Acts 18:7. In Rom. 16:23 Paul calls him Gaius (evidently his prænomen) as in I Cor. 1:14.

[7] Deissmann, *St. Paul*, pp. 235–60.

Chapter XI

[1] See Num. 6:13–18.

[2] See I Cor. 11:2–16; II Cor. 11:7.

[8] While Acts records a brief visit to Jerusalem at this point in Paul's movements, this can hardly have taken place

or Paul would not have passed it over in silence in listing
his visits to the church there in Gal. 1:13 to 2:14. Luke
evidently assumed that Paul would not have failed to pay
his respects to the Jerusalem leaders before visiting Antioch,
but Paul was not yet ready to fulfil his promise of financial
aid for the Jerusalem poor, made at the council visit of Gal.
2:1; Acts, ch. 15. He had indeed helped in such an effort in
Antioch years before and had plans for such a contribution
from his western churches, but no funds as yet to turn over.
If he had just come from Jerusalem when he wrote Galatians, as Acts implies, he could hardly have failed to mention
it in Gal., ch. 2.

⁴ Col. 3:22–25.
⁶ Like Hermas of Rome, ca. A.D. 100, and his brother
Pius, later ninth bishop of Rome.

Chapter XII

¹ A part of this letter is probably preserved in II Cor. 6:14
to 7:1, for it interrupts the context in II Corinthians and
deals with the subject of the lost first letter, as Paul gives it
in I Cor. 5:9.
² I Cor. 7:1.
³ Paul Elmer More.

Chapter XIII

¹ Grenfell, Hunt and Goodspeed, *Tebtunis Papyri*, II,
papyrus 275 is a good example—a charm for protection from
fever, addressed to a deity called Kok Kouk Koul and preceded by a long magical word of thirty-four letters, repeated in successive lines with the successive omissions of

the first and last letters until only the central letter "a" remains, the whole forming an inverted triangle which must have been very difficult to utter, and quite meaningless as well.

Chapter XIV

[1] Paul's despairing language in II Cor. 1:8–10 does not suggest a period of imprisonment in Ephesus, as some interpreters suppose. It reflects a far more bitter and devastating experience. Paul had no such feeling about being shut up in prison; he had a religious philosophy which was more than equal to such tests. It was the apparent defection of the Corinthians that had stung him and hurt him so deeply. This betrayal by his own converts for whom he had gone through so much and worked so hard cut him to the heart.

Chapter XV

[1] It is usually assumed from the language of Acts 20:2, 3 that this journey from Macedonia to Corinth and back was made by land, but that would have taken so much longer than going by ship that it may be dismissed as most unlikely. It was evidently late in the autumn, and the three months in Corinth were clearly the winter months, December, January, February, Acts 20:5,6. Even so, the voyage from Thessalonica to Corinth, even if taken in November, was a series of coast journeys, much of it by an inner route and more feasible than the long, winding land journey, much of it mountainous and hence doubly difficult in winter. The stages of such a supposed land journey may be figured roughly as:

Berea to Larissa	four days
Larissa to Pharsalus by way of Volo or direct, the way Pompey came in 48 B.C. to meet Cæsar, more than thirty miles	two days
Pharsalus to Lamia, thirty-five miles	two days
Lamia to Livadia, 18½ hours	three days
Livadia to Thebes, 7 hours, twenty-five miles	one day
Thebes to Athens, forty-four miles	two days
Athens to Corinth, sixty miles	three days

—a total of at least seventeen days, sure to be extended in winter travel with snow and rain to three weeks. The sea journey, roughly four hundred miles, by the inner route, sheltered by the long island of Euboea, could hardly exceed a week in duration, besides being much less arduous. The return to Macedonia in March by way of Athens, Thebes, Livadia, Lamia, Pharsalus and Larissa to Berea and Thessalonica seems to me equally improbable. Even if mounted, as Paul seldom was, his progress would not ordinarily exceed twenty to twenty-four miles a day, for six to seven hours in the saddle is all anyone not a cavalryman can reasonably do day after day on mountain roads and trails.

[2] The probability that ch. 16 is not a real part of the letter to the Romans was enhanced by the publication in 1935 of the Chester Beatty papyrus of Paul, a manuscript written not long after A.D. 200, which places the great doxology of Rom. 16:25–7 at the end of ch. 15. Most manuscripts place it after ch. 16, some after ch. 14, a few in both places, but

the testimony of this oldest of our manuscripts of Paul seems to explain all the other readings. Certainly it encourages the view that ch. 16 was not addressed to the Romans. It would be strange if Paul knew so many members of the church at Rome, where he had never been, still more strange that he knows their domestic groupings, and their various house congregations—that is, in whose houses church groups were meeting. Strange, too, is the presence in Rome of Prisca and Aquila, whom Paul had left in Ephesus, and the presence there of Epænetus, the first man in Asia to accept the gospel; we should expect to find him in Ephesus. Paul's familiarity with the Christian records of a number of the people to whom he sends his greetings is strange too. Some of them have shown him great personal kindness. Surely all this adds up to a church with which he has worked a long time, like Ephesus. He would be much more likely to introduce Phoebe to such a church than to one he has never seen. A woman of Cenchreae is more likely to have contacts and interests about the Ægean than the Adriatic, and short voyages are more probable than long ones. The brevity of Paul's religious message, vs. 17–19, accords with his having been with them until recently—he has little to add to what he has been teaching them so lately—and has a slightly casual sound: "Everyone has heard of your obedience and I am very happy about you, but I want you to be wise about what is good and guileless about what is bad." If this is Paul's last word to the Romans, we would expect him to say something much more incisive, restating the main thesis of his letter, like his closing word in Galatians, 6:11–17.

³ Deut., ch. 28.

Chapter XVI

[1] There is good reason for accepting Luke, the Greek doctor of Col. 4:14 (Philemon 24; II Tim. 4:11), as Paul's traveling companion and the writer of The Acts. In the first place, if he is not the writer, why has tradition fixed upon him for these rôles? He is one of the most obscure persons in the whole story, and his name carried no apostolic or ecclesiastical weight. He is never mentioned in the Apostolic Fathers or the pre-Catholic Apologists, and only most casually in Philemon and II Timothy. The fact that The Acts shows no special medical element in its vocabulary, shows only that like Dr. Oliver Wendell Holmes the writer knew how to lay aside his technical terms when he wrote for the public. The immense improbability of the old "we-sections" theory, which would convict the editor of The Acts of making the same mistake of copying first persons which he should have changed to thirds the incredible number of seventy-seven times in using the imaginary "we" diary, is obvious. But if Luke did not keep that record and write The Acts from it, we have to conjecture just such another figure, a Greek companion of Paul's travels and prisons, educated and alert, capable of being the Christian logographer the writer of The Acts was. It is, of course, natural that the earliest gospels written by Jewish Christians should be anonymous; Jewish books tended to be so. But not Greek books. The Greek sense of authorship was so keen that a single epigram a few lines long could immortalize its writer's name. And Luke-Acts had an author; it was not just a social product. He must have named himself, for he gave his book a preface telling of his purpose and sources, and a

dedication to Theophilus, a strange thing to do if it was anonymous. At appropriate points in his two volumes he uses the first person, with perfect propriety, Luke 1:3; Acts 1:1, and it is closing our eyes to plain facts to suppose that in Acts 16:10–18; 20:5–16; 21:1–18; 27:1 to 28:16 he does not still mean just what he says. No one who has patiently compared every line of the Greek Gospel of Luke with the Greek Gospel of Mark and observed the painstaking care of the writer of Luke in his use of Mark can suppose him capable of such a riot of blunders. His almost unfailing adherence to Mark in the order of the sections of his narrative further illustrates his fidelity to his sources.

As a companion of Paul's journeys, and near him in his imprisonment in Cæsarea and his winter in Malta, the author not only heard some of his speeches but had abundant opportunity to learn much from Paul about his journeys, speeches and great moments, memories of which could and did enrich his narrative when years afterwards the idea of his book on the beginnings of Christianity came to Luke. These he wrote, of course, from the point of view of that later day when the Judaizing problem had disappeared and a more eccleciastical view of the church was emerging, and with no such keen sense of the heart of Paulinism as the letters of Paul reveal.

[2] Luke 13:33.

Chapter XVII

[1] Josephus, *Wars of the Jews*, II, 12 and 13.
[2] Matt. 24:18; Mark 13:16; Luke 17:31.

Chapter XVIII

[1] It is perfectly natural for Luke to embellish his narrative with snatches of conversation, for nothing lives more vividly in the memory of the actors in such scenes than what was said in these tense moments, and it would be less than natural if Paul had not repeated some such conversations and remarks, in the course of his voyages with Luke, his being shut up with him for three winter months in Malta, and his imprisonments at Cæsarea and Rome. This is particularly true of an interchange of words like this one, in which Paul may be thought to have had the worst of it.

Chapter XIX

[1] Col. 1:24.

[2] The year before he had written to the Corinthians that he had been shipwrecked three times, II Cor. 11:25.

[3] On Paul's right as he approached the city the giant arches of the Aqua Claudia, the Claudian aqueduct, then recently completed, must have met his eyes, and he passed close to the huge old tomb of Cæcilia Metella not long before his party went through the Appian Gate.

Chapter XX

[1] Heb. 6:10; 10:33, 34.

[2] Wisdom 9:1, 2, 9.

[3] Col. 1:24.

[4] Against the identification of Philemon with the letter from Laodicea, long ago advanced by Wieseler as scarcely open to doubt, Abbott, *Epistles to the Ephesians and to the*

Colossians, ICC, p. 306, says: "That epistle is entirely private, and the delicacy of its appeal would be destroyed if St. Paul directed it to be read in public."—Abbott evidently forgets that Philemon itself is specifically addressed to Philemon, Apphia, Archippus "and the church that meets in your house." Having the letter read to the Colossian church would be no more indelicate than having it read to the Laodicean church, in Philemon's house.

⁵ The pastoral letters, to Timothy and Titus, are plainly from another hand than Paul's and belong to another period, when the sects were in full swing, soon after A.D. 150. Their vigorous attacks upon the sects reflect the times of Marcionism and Gnosticism; the end of I Timothy actually mentions Marcion's book, the *Contradictions*, by name. They show the need of uniformity among the churches about their officers and their qualifications for office. They reverse Marcion's rejection of the Old Testament, II Tim. 3:16, and rescue Paul's letters, which Marcion had adopted and made part of his Scripture, by describing Paul as repudiating Marcion's views, and offering the churches these three letters as a supplement to the Pauline collection. Their references to further journeys of Paul between two Roman imprisonments are based on the fact that the end of Acts leaves the matter of his conviction open, but they make no serious contribution to our knowledge of Paul's life.

Chapter XXI

¹ The ancients were no strangers to the search for written literary materials. At the beginning of his Gospel Luke indicates that he has made use of a number of sources, and

modern study has distinguished at least four or five in that volume. It is unlikely that they fell into his hands without any searching on his part. Not much more than a century later Origen succeeded in finding three anonymous Greek versions of the Old Testament besides those of Aquila, Theodotion and Symmachus. Later still, Jerome was a discoverer of manuscripts. Particularly in the case of the personal letters of some distinguished figure such a course would be inevitable. They had been dispatched in all directions and must be looked for in as many quarters.

[2] See Albert E. Barnett, *Paul Becomes a Literary Influence.* 1941.

[3] Heb. 5:12.

BOOKS ABOUT PAUL

Conybeare and Howson, *The Life and Epistles of St. Paul*. 2 vols. 1854 and often since.

Ramsay, W. M., *St. Paul the Traveller and the Roman Citizen*. 1896.

Bacon, B. W., *The Story of St. Paul*. 1904.

McNeile, A. H., *St. Paul; His Life, Letters, and Christian Doctrine*. 1920.

Deissmann, Adolf, *St. Paul: A Study in Social and Religious History*. 1926.

Foakes-Jackson, F. J., *The Life of Saint Paul, the Man and the Apostle*. 1926.

Robinson, B. W., *The Life of Paul*. 1928.

Glover, T. R., *Paul of Tarsus*. 1930.

Enslin, M. S., *The Ethics of Paul*. 1930.

Scott, C. A. A., *St. Paul: The Man and the Teacher*. 1936.

Nock, A. D., *St. Paul*. 1938.

Riddle, Donald W., *Paul, Man of Conflict*. 1940.

Weiss, Johannes, *The History of Primitive Christianity*. Completed by Rudolf Knopf. Translated and edited by Frederick C. Grant. 1937.

INDEX

A

Abraham, 108–109
Acts of the Apostles, 215, 235–236
Address at Athens, 87–88
Address before Agrippa, 183–186
Address to the mob, 170
Agabus, 161
Age of Paul, 224
Agrippa II, 182–186
Alexander, 3, 67, 73
Alexandria, 113, 150
Altar to unknown God, 88, 229–230
Amphipolis, 81
Ananias, 21
Ananias, high priest, 173, 176, 181
Antioch (Pisidian), 44, 46, 51, 69, 113
Antioch (Syrian), 30–33, 35–37, 38, 51, 57, 60, 62, 64, 102–104, 106, 212
Antipatris, 176
Anti-Semitism, 83
Aphrodite, 40

Apocrypha, 114
Apollos, 113–115, 117, 122, 150
Apostleship, 106
Appeal to Cæsar, 181
Appearance, Paul's, 225
Apphia, 208
Appian Way, 148, 195–198, 206
Aquila, 91–92, 102, 114–116, 129, 146
Arabia, 21–22
Aramaic, 4–6, 27, 169
Aratus, 89
Archippus, 208
Areopagus, 87
Aretas, 24
Aristarchus, 137, 188
Artemis, 115, 136
Astarte, 40
Athenodorus, 3
Athens, 86–89
Augustus, 1, 91

B

Barnabas, 26, 30–51, 53, 54, 62–65, 104
Beatings, 24

Berea, 84
Bernice, 182

C

Cæsarea, 160–161, 176–177
Catalog of hardships, 131–132, 142
Cenchreae, 145, 153–155
Cephas, see Peter
Chloe, 117–118, 122, 128
Christ, 18, 19, 35 and often
Cicero, 196
Cilician cloth, 11
Cilician Gates, 67
Circumcision, 1, 55, 58, 59, 104
Cleanthes, 230
Clement, I, 210, 218
Collection of the letters, 216–217
Colossæ, 204–210
Colossians, Letter to, 204–210
Conversion, 18–20
Copper, 39–40
Corinth, 90, 102, 145, 148
Corinthians, I, 19, 101, 120–127, 128
Corinthians, II, 24, 131, 141–144
Council meeting, 55–59
Crete, 189–190
Crispus, 99, 101

Cumanus, 160, 163–164
Cyprus, 30, 38–43, 65

D

Damascus, 17–18, 20–22, 24, 25
Delphi inscription, 100
Demetrius, 136
Derbe, 49–50, 51, 68, 113
Destination of Rom., chapter 16, 233–234
Dio Cassius, 100
Dionysius of Corinth, 210
Distress in Ephesus, 138
Dress of women, 121, 124
Drusilla, 178

E

Ecstatic speaking, 121, 125
Egnatian Way, 81, 84
Epaphras, 204, 207
Epaphroditus, 197–198, 202–203
Ephesia Grammata, 135
Ephesians, Letter to, 216
Ephesus, 102–103, 114–116, 134, 137, 138, 145–146, 210, 213
Europe, 72–73, 80
Eusebius, 211

F

Faith, 56, 58, 152
Felix, 160, 164, 176–180

Festus, 179–180, 184
Food restrictions, 60–61
Freedom, 109–110

G

Gaius (of Corinth), 154, 230
Gaius (of Derbe), 137
Gaius of Rome, 211
Galatia, 42, 46, 51, 57, 65, 68–69, 104–105
Galatians, Letter to, 19, 43, 45, 58, 63, 81, 106–112, 166
Gallio, 99, 100
Gamaliel, 10, 16
Gospels, 212
Greek culture, 34
Greek papyri, 136

H

Halakhah, 8
Hebrew, 4
Hebrew in synagogues, 223
Hebrews, 217–218
Hecataeus, 179
Herod Agrippa I, 55, 178
Herodotus, 179
Hogarth, D. G., 227
Horace, 196
Hymn to Apollo, 73

I

Iconium, 47, 51, 69, 113
Ignatius, 210, 218–219

Influence on theology, 221
Issus, 67

J

Jailer of Philippi, 77–78
James, brother of Jesus, 26–27, 55, 58–61, 64, 107, 166
Jason, 83
Jerusalem, 10, 14–17, 54–61, 107, 162–171, 174–175
Jerusalem fund, 142–145, 149, 155–156
Jesus, 1 and often
Jewish Law, 6–8, 107–108
Jewish missions, 52–53
Johannists, 114–115
John, 55, 58
John, Gospel of, 218
John, Paul's influence on, 220
John the Baptist, 114
Jonathan, high priest, 164
Josephus, 10, 165, 192, 236
Judaizers, 54–65, 69, 104–105, 200
Judas Barsabbas, 66
Julius, 188–190, 193, 196
Juvenal, 33
Justus, Titius, 99, 230

K

Kinsmen, 6

L

Laodicea, 206–210, 237–238
Lawsuits, 118

Letter of introduction, 145
Letter from Corinth, 119
Letters of Paul, 213, 215–219
Logos, 114
Lord's Supper, 118, 157
Love, 125
Luke, 55, 71–74, 80, 157–159, 161, 166, 178, 188, 196, 206, 210, 213
Lydia, 75–76, 80
Lysias, Claudius, 168–171, 173–177
Lystra, 30, 47–51, 68

M

Maccabees, I, 11
Maccabees, II, 12
Macedonia, 81, 92
Magical texts, 135
Malaria, 50, 71
Malta, 192–195, 236, 237
Mark, 35–36, 42–43, 65, 206
Mark, Gospel of, 213
Marriage, 120, 122
Martyrdom, 210–211, 213
Mary's house, 36
Matthew, 212
Mela, 100
Miletus, 158
Mishna, 7
Mnason, 162

N

Nero, 100, 211

O

Onesimus, 206–210
Origen, 211
Orosius, 230
Ovid, 48

P

Palestine, 103
Paphos, 40–41
Pastoral letters, 238
Paul's name, 3–5, 41
Paulus, Sergius, 40–41, 227–228
Pausanias, 229
Perga, 42–44, 51
Peter, 26–27, 58–64, 118, 122
Pharisees, 7, 10, 12–14, 19, 21, 174
Philemon, 206–210
Philip, 160–161
Philip of Macedon, 74
Philippi, 72, 74–80, 145, 156, 158, 196–204
Philippians, Letter to, 29, 200–204
Philo, 114
Phoebe, 215
Pliny, 100, 194
Pliny the Younger, 216
Polycarp, 218, 219
Priscilla, 76, 92, 102, 114–116, 146

Ptolemais, 160
Puteoli, 195

Q

Quadratus, 164

R

Relief visit, 35, 37
Release at Philippi, 78–79
Resurrection, 126, 174
Revelation, 217–219
Riot in Ephesus, 136–137
Roman citizenship, 3, 10, 79,
    170–171, 176, 181, 211
Romans, Letter to, 19, 149–
    154,.155, 211
Rome, 148, 150, 174, 210–
    212

S

Sadducees, 56
Salamis, 40
Sardis, 70, 71
Seneca, 99–100, 195
Sergius Paulus, 40–41, 227–
    228
Sermon on the Mount, 12
Sicarii, 160, 164–165
Silvanus (Silas), 65–67, 73,
    77, 84, 87, 89, 91–95
Slavery, 111, 206–210
Soli, 40–41
Sosthenes, 100–101

Spain, 147–148
Stephanas, 119, 127, 154
Stephen, 13–17
Stoic preachers, 33
Stoning, 14–15, 49
Suetonius, 230
Syrian Gates, 66–67

T

Tacitus, 100
Talmud, 7
Tarsus, 2–8, 29, 31–32, 67,
    169
Taurus Mountains, 67
Temple meat, 120, 122–123
Tertullian, 210
Thecla, 228
Thessalonians, I, 66, 82, 93–
    97, 100
Thessalonians, II, 66, 98
Thessalonica, 81, 83–87, 145,
    156
Tiberius, 2, 115
Timothy, 68–69, 73, 87, 89,
    91–96, 100, 135, 156, 166,
    206
Timothy and Titus, Letters
    to, 219
Titius Justus, 99, 230. See
    Gaius (of Corinth)
Titus, 54, 57, 69, 133–134,
    136, 138–143
Tolerance, 153

INDEX

Trade, 10, 11, 84, 116
Troas, 69, 71, 134, 138, 156, 158
Trophimus, 156, 167
Tychicus, 156, 166, 178, 206
Tyrannus, 115, 127–128
Tyre, 159–160

V

Vegetius, 194
Ventriloquism, 76–77
Venus, 40

W

Wisdom, Book of, 114, 150, 205
Women in religion, 76, 111
Women's dress, 121

X

Xenophon, 67–68, 70

Z

Zeus, 30, 230